CATCH YOUR BREATH!

EXHALING DEATH & INHALING LIFE

BARRY L. CALLEN

ALDERSGATE
PRESS

CATCH YOUR BREATH!
By Barry L. Callen

Copyright © 2014 Barry L. Callen

All rights reserved. No part of this book may be reproduced, or stored in a retrieval system or transmitted in any form or by any means, electronic, mechanical, photocopying, recording, scanning or otherwise, except as permitted by the 1976 United States Copyright Act, or with the prior written permission of Aldersgate Press. Requests for permission should be addressed to the editor of Aldersgate Press, *Editor@AldersgatePress.com*.

Unless otherwise noted, all scripture quotations are from the New Revised Standard Version Bible, copyright © 1989 the Division of Christian Education of the National Council of the Churches of Christ in the United States of America. Used by permission. All rights reserved.

ALDERSGATE **PRESS**
THE PUBLICATIONS ARM OF

HolinessandUnity.org

In Collaboration with

 **LAMP POST inc.**
www.lamppostpublishers.com
Spring Valley, CA

Printed in the United States of America

Hard Cover ISBN-13:   978-1-60039-302-0
Soft Cover ISBN 13:   978-1-60039-301-3
    ebook ISBN-13:   978-1-60039-975-6

Library of Congress Control Number: 2014942294

TABLE OF CONTENTS

Preface .... *v*
1. Go For It—Now! 1

Letting Go: Exhaling **15**
2. Finding the Right Agenda 17
3. Movements Good and Bad 27
4. Going Back Is Moving Forward 39
5. Can We Be "Perfect"? 51
6. But Not So Fast 71
7. Rhythms of the Spirit 89

Letting God: Inhaling **101**
8. Living in the Right House 103
9. Exercising "Means" of Grace 119
10. Available Breathing Plans 139
11. Even When It Hurts 159
12. Embracing the Beyond 177

Endnotes *195*

PREFACE

The earth was a formless void and darkness covered the face of the deep, while a wind from God swept over the face of the waters (Gen. 1:2).

If God did not exist, it would be necessary to invent Him.
—Voltaire

These two quotes say it all. Creation was nothing until the breath of God swept over the waters and that which was without form and densely dark took shape and blazed with light! The simple fact is that we all need such shape and light, the life that comes only from God breathing graciously and creatively. If we deny this, reject God, the good only comes—we hope—when we try to replace God, or invent him as Voltaire once put it. Somehow we must catch our breath in order to really live.

There is no question that people today are gasping for air. They are spiritually hungry, starved for the oxygen of some good and truly life-giving spirit. Empty lungs are an awful thing, much like the "formless void and darkness" seen at the beginning of creation. Ironically, what is not being accepted today is "the wind of God" that can fill what is empty and bring life where there is only death. We moderns need to catch our breath—God's breath!

The issue is where to find the good air that can fill desperate lungs and be satisfying food for the soul. The purely secular arena, life without God in the picture, is just too empty to do the job. Invent as we will, suffocation is still everywhere. Here's a prominent writer of today saying this very thing, although he still wants to proceed without God. You will forgive me for giving a modern atheist the first word—I assure you that his will not be the last. I have reference to a very popular 2012 book titled *Religion for Atheists* by Alain de Botton.

The *San Francisco Chronicle* calls this book "wonderfully dangerous and subversive." Subversive means that it deliberately seeks to undercut the secular delusion that tossing out religion with the childish trash of yesterday is coming at much too high a human price. The author, non-religious in any standard sense, argues with courage that "it must be possible to remain a committed atheist and nevertheless find religions sporadically useful, interesting, and consoling—and be curious as to the possibilities of importing certain of their ideas and practices into the secular realm."[1]

Why does this author call for some importing from a source judged as alien as traditional religion? Simple. Seculars are still spiritually hungry, missing something important after their God-denial. Some of them are now coming to realize and admit openly the emptiness of their spiritual lungs. Our secular author explains: "God may be dead, but the urgent issues which impelled us to make him up still stir and demand resolutions.... Religions understand the value of training our minds with rigor that we [seculars] are accustomed to applying only to the training of our bodies. They present us with an array of spiritual exercises designed to strengthen our inclinations towards virtuous thoughts and patterns of behavior."[2]

PREFACE

These present pages come from within traditional Christianity. God is still gratefully acknowledged in all that follows, and it is assumed that our spiritual needs are very real and can be satisfied only by the cleansing and empowering grace of a loving God. Even so, something from our secular author rings true and brings judgment into our religious camp. The very thing that he admires and longs for in religion is what so many Christians are virtually ignoring in their own faith practice—putting them closer to the hungry secularist than they would care to admit.

There are two ironies here, both sad and suffocating. One is that "liberated" seculars still find themselves bound by a breathless emptiness that is deadening. The other is that many traditional Christians are also spiritually hungry and breathless. They may have believed all the right things, but have not breathed in the powerful, re-creating, lung-filling wind of God's Spirit.

> As non-believers reach in hunger for the treasures of Christian faith, may we who do believe not forfeit those very treasures by our breathless and tragic inaction!

Without denying anything about the existence and sovereignty and love of God, it remains the case that there is "an array of spiritual exercises" designed and provided by God to strengthen the inclinations of believers towards "virtuous thoughts and patterns of behavior" (holiness). These exercises, when understood biblically, are hardly self-help means of getting into heaven. Even so, they are practices critical to the realization of a matured holiness that is essential for being God's intended children in this world—and maybe even for managing a heavenly entrance later. They assist us with the process of exhaling death and inhaling new life.

As non-believers reach in hunger for the treasures of Christian faith, may we who do believe not forfeit those very treasures by our breathless and tragic inaction! Let's catch our breath spiritually, open our windows to the wind of God. As we do, let's never forget the necessary context required by the Spirit-wind:

> God's grace facilitates people's freedom to choose or not to choose to cooperate with divine grace. God…makes it possible for us to love God as well as to reject God. Such grace neither diminishes the sovereignty of God nor gives people responsibility apart from the empowering work of the Holy Spirit.… It requires people to think and act in responsible ways, always cognizant that they do so by divine grace.[3]

So, we do all by divine grace. We catch the wind of God only because it chooses to blow our way. What we must do is seek in faith, set our sails to catch the wind, and begin to breath in, cooperating and acting responsibly. We are given a divine gift, the potential of new life, and we must accept it and then be actively responsible with it.

"Holiness" may be thought of as our having really caught our (God's) breath again. It is the experience of re-filled lungs. Death is exhaled and the Spirit is inhaled deeply. Holiness certainly is far less *something achieved* and much more *Someone received*. Even so, once God has been gracious to us and become present within, it clearly becomes time for us to *breath deeply*—and regularly and deeply. God provides the means for spiritual growth. We must actively engage those means—and live again!

CHAPTER 1

GO FOR IT—*NOW!*

Pursue [now!] peace with everyone, and the holiness without which no one will see the Lord (Heb. 12:14).

The problem of human existence is that our immense appetite for the divine has been tragically misdirected, turned in on itself, satiated with transient goods. To redirect and redeem fallen humanity, God became man in the person of His Son, Jesus Christ. Yet so "long as Christ remains *outside* of us, and we are separated from him, all that he has suffered and done... remains useless and of no value for us."[4]

Holiness is essential—and it happens only when Christ comes *inside* us, when his Spirit is breathed in and applies the benefits of Christ's work. Here should be our desperate prayer: "Father, if thou my Father art, Send forth the Spirit of thy Son, Breathe him into my panting heart."[5]

When you need to catch your breath, there's no time to waste! So let's get right to a core question. Is it true that no one will even see the Lord without being holy? This is what Hebrews says (12:4). Then let's go for it—and right away! But what is "it" (being holy) and how do we go wherever it is? Maybe reporting on a near tragedy will help bring an answer.

It is hard to imagine a more terrible scene. The little body is just floating helplessly below the surface of the family's backyard pool. A neighbor sees and screams for the father, who is inside the house thinking that others are supervising the fun-loving boy. Within seconds, Dad has the little boy out of the water, frantically working on his limp body. Suddenly, despair flees as a gush of fluid flies out of the little mouth and the boy begins breathing again. Dead? No. Saved!!

Actively Receiving God's Gift

This pool-side picture dramatizes life having gone away and then suddenly coming back again. It illustrates the life-giving, life-sustaining, double process of exhaling, clearing the killer blockage, and then inhaling, taking in the air that renewed life requires. It illustrates key aspects of God's working with dying sinners, encouraging them to pursue holiness—actual life in God's Spirit. Holiness is resurrected life, catching God's breath that renews life in the image of Jesus.

The lack of adequate supervision and the surprised and frantically running of Dad do not apply, of course. God always knows our condition and, although deeply saddened over our fallenness, is never desperate. But the rest of it does apply. God knows what is necessary for our salvaging ("salvation") and acts graciously on behalf of life. We must learn what is required of us to receive the divine gift and cultivate the new spiritual life. That is where our "exercising" comes in.

Since our heavenly Father gets to us in our desperation and does crucial work while we are yet helpless, this terrible scene of near drowning makes clear that all new spiritual life is a gift of God, the result of the love of God rushing to our sides and making breathing possible again. But there is more. After God's initial work, the ongoing health of the new life becomes dependent in significant part on our doing the necessary follow-up things, exercising our air-hungry lungs, benefitting from the gracious gift of our Father, and cultivating what is now alive again.

Here is the fundamental fact that creates the crisis in the first place. Sin blocks our spiritual breath. It must be *exhaled* by God's grace and power before we can *inhale* the amazing and life-returning breath of God. Out and in, holy initiative and human response, holiness exercises and wonderful new life. Such exercising is both the gift of God's Spirit and then the privilege and work of every disciple of Jesus.

Sequence is important if we are to face the real consequences of our sin—and keep our theology straight. We first are enabled by God's sheer grace to expel the deadly blockage—God rescues (Rom. 6:24-25). Then, with fresh breathing enabled, we must take initiative and see to it that sin no longer exercises dominion in our bodies (Rom. 6:13). Grace cannot be *possessed*, but it can be received again and again. However, it will sour if received and not put to good use—like exercising it toward the ending of the dominion of sin in our lives.

> God rushes to our limp, sin-choked bodies, lovingly performs a saving miracle, and announces, "Breathe, my child. You can do it. I am here to help. Let out that killer water and take in the fresh air of my Spirit. Let there be life. Live again!"

God makes possible the renewal of life, and then we are to take responsibility for our renewed spiritual lives. God acts first and then we must "exercise" in response. We are instructed to strive, stretch, strain, and sweat as necessary in pursuit of the holiness without which no one will see the Lord (Heb. 12:14). God provides; we then must be active, grateful, disciplined receivers. To use the language of John Calvin above, we must not keep Jesus Christ *outside* us, but breathe in his Spirit so that we can come to enjoy Christ and all his benefits.

Millions of Americans flock to gyms and health clubs these days. They often are armed with New Year's resolutions about getting in shape. Medical experts are on their side about the wisdom of this. That is, there is wisdom in vigorous exercise if people follow through and avoid overdoing. Regular workouts may help fight off colds and flu, reduce the risk of certain cancers and chronic diseases, and even slow the process of aging. Exercise can bring fresh hope—although you first need a body that is alive. First, we must catch our breath!

Measured and regular physical activity has long been known to bestow benefits, such as helping to maintain a healthy weight and reduce stress, not to mention tightening those flabby abs. A growing body of research is now showing that regular exercise—as simple as a brisk 30 to 45 minute walk five times a week—can boost the body's immune system, increasing the circulation of natural killer cells that fight off viruses and bacteria. I said, regular exercise. There is danger. A sudden burst of intense activity after a long period of none can tear muscles and even bring on a heart attack or stroke.

Life in the Spirit, according to the physically departing Jesus, is God's future already active in the present (Acts 1:5, 8). We believers are to catch our spiritual breath, the Spirit's enlivening and empowering breath, and we are to do it now!

What about spiritual activity? At birth, it often is necessary to clear the throat and lungs of the baby so that the natural breathing process can begin in the dramatic new world outside the womb. What the Bible calls "sin" is much like that—and we all have it. Entering God's kingdom, being re-born, regenerated, requires a clearing of the clogged spiritual lungs. Dad (God) rushes to our limp, sin-choked bodies, lovingly performs a saving miracle, and announces, "Breathe, my child. You can do it. I am here to help. Let out that killer water and take in the fresh air of my Spirit. Let there be life. Live again!"

Unfortunately, we do not always respond properly. Sin has a tight grip, even a death grip on us. I shudder when recalling a scene I once witnessed in a hospital room. Smoking restrictions wouldn't allow this now, but then it actually happened. A man nearing death from emphysema was in the bed—smoking! The oxygen tank was right there, but he had removed the mask long enough to have just one more cigarette. The habit already killing him was so strong that he stopped breathing the life-sustaining oxygen long enough to destroy his lungs just a little bit more—and risk blowing up the entire room in the process!

Breathing is huge for us fragile humans. Exhaling and inhaling form an essential rhythm for enabling and sustaining life. This also is true of the Christian spiritual life. We must exhale death—the old sinful self—and inhale the new self that God wants to provide. This is the breathing necessary for holiness to become real. Christian holiness is the subject of this book, and holiness is certainly the goal of our faith lives. Specific ways for ongoing spiritual health will be suggested later. First, increased understanding of "holiness" is necessary.

While "holiness" has several definitions that will be explored later, we must be clear about one thing from the beginning. Holiness, the goal and character of Christian life at its best, is the wonderful God-life that can be present within us. It is the result of God's gracious awakening of sinful humans and of those humans then taking some responsibility for their own spiritual growth and health. We must actively exhale the old and inhale the new breath of life. This whole process is critical in the moment of rebirth and essential for the lifetime of faith.

Having holiness grafted deeply into our lives is both the result of God's initial work and then of our necessary responding work. We are to engage in breathing in the oxygen of the Spirit that completes the activation of this spiritual resurrection. New-life breathing is always a matter of divine grace—but it is also a matter of our intentional cooperation with that grace. We receive and we exercise. In fact, regular breathing in and out is required for continued reception of the divine gift of the holy life.

No Despair, No Default

Breathing is basic, of course. But timing is also a big deal. When I watch a skilled football quarterback throw a pass, I marvel at the split-second timing required for success. It must be a throw to a spot on the field where the running receiver will be at the instant the football arrives. The quarterback, in faith, throws where no one yet is, believing that, if thrown well and if the receiver runs the right route, the future on the other end will be a big gain, maybe even a touchdown.

When we think about more theological subjects like heaven, the timing issue also becomes plain. So many Christians tend to make the wrong timing choice. They opt for *then* at the expense of *now*. They despair about the present and decide not to throw the football at all, fearing that it might be intercepted or that the receiver cannot be trusted to be in just the right spot at precisely the right time. Heaven becomes a dream, a hope, even a preoccupation that parks the present in neutral and freezes the throwing hand in mid-air.

Faith easily gets focused on *then*, leaving the *now* to its sinful, choking mess. Holiness becomes only a far-away hope that we believe will happen without our present action—which would be useless. Nothing that we can do now will help. All must be from the hand of the gracious God. This world of ours is out of control and cannot be turned around except by the return of Christ. Our personal sin is so deep that it will take death, maybe some kind of purgatory, to ever get us ready for a holy heaven.

This thinking is not all wrong, just not all right. Heaven is ahead, yes, and we are helpless apart from divine grace. That part is accurate.

Even so, we easily forget that God's will is to be done *on earth* as well as in heaven (Matt. 6:10). Our failure to receive and act in the present features a devastating default that grows out of too much despairing and passive waiting. What could be *now* gets thrown away as we wait for what we hope *will be* (Heaven) and will not be for us (Hell). God's grace is judged not sufficient for today. Only later will it be possible for us to become "holy."

Since sin is known to have a solid foothold now, we presume that holiness cannot be for today. It must wait until we breathe our last, or Christ returns in a refining blaze of glory, or we arrive in some purgatory where real cleansing finally gets done. So we hold the football in our nervous hands and, without throwing it, hope that somehow it will get caught down the field in the great by and by. Holiness is delayed, thought of as only a later in-heaven thing. We default on our spiritual privileges by doing more *waiting* than working, more *hoping* than helping, more *brooding* than breathing in the life of God.

That is the confusion of our mortal clocks. We believers commonly make the wrong timing choice. We are wanting to be sure of what will *not* be after our deaths. Being heavily preoccupied with the eventual consequences of sin, we shape our present faith lives around avoiding the hell that lurks out there beyond this life for unrepentant sinners. Believing in Christ becomes essentially a buying of "fire insurance," making sure that we are protected from the extreme heat of the negative world that we presume awaits most people. It is thought better to hold the football, even be "sacked" for now, and wait for the possible miracles of later plays in the next season when God will be fully in charge of the game and all mouths will have to confess that Jesus really is Lord (Phil. 2:11).

The core of this wrong timing choice is this: what might happen in the far future dominates today's life to the point that faith loses its trust in what God wants to accomplish and is more than able to accomplish *in the now*. Preparing only for later cripples the life to be lived now. Thinking properly about holiness—not putting it off until later—can pull the believer into a joyful confidence in God's present intentions and provisions for life that is to be received and lived *on this side of eternity*.

Here is wisdom that points us in the right direction. What happened at Pentecost (Acts 2) provides the connecting link between past and present, then and now. The continuity between the historical presence of Jesus and our present salvation was disclosed in the living presence of the Spirit of Christ. Life in the Spirit, according to the physically departing Jesus, is God's future already active in the present (Acts 1:5, 8). We believers are to catch our spiritual breath, the Spirit's enlivening and empowering breath, and we are to do it now!

At Pentecost, God's breath burst on that ancient scene. Resurrection life moved from Jesus to his disciples through the Spirit so that those spiritually dead were enabled by the power of God's sheer grace to exhale the old life of sin and begin inhaling the new life of the divine—immediately. The Spirit of God is the divine presence of possibility in the face of every impossibility. It is the same wind of God that first blew over that dark void and brought to creation light and life. It fills our lungs, dances on our heads, and sends us into the world celebrating and proclaiming.

Holiness often is understood as the goal to be realized only in the great beyond. It is seen through the eyes of *despair* that leads to current *default*. But biblical holiness is not to be reduced to our becoming isolated in bomb shelters of faith that are thought to bring safety from the coming nuclear war of sin's horrible consequences. "Salvation," one might say, is a shelter from the storm, but hardly *only* that—and only *then*.

A glorified spiritual perfection will indeed come only when the limits of this world's compromised existence are transcended. Still, Christian holiness is a call to live boldly, by God's enabling grace, as examples of spiritual transformation here and now, right where the sin danger still is, and right where God currently is at work on behalf of this present and very broken world.

Easter rejoicing should not be allowed to ignore the Pentecost follow-through. Those first disciples of Jesus waited in Jerusalem as they had been told to do, and soon they knew why. The Spirit was to come and help them to exhale and then inhale the very breath of God—essential preparation for effective mission.

Christian holiness is as much gaining a participation in the life of God *now* as it is waiting for that divine life to appear in its fullness *later*. We must honor both the "from" and "for" words essential to the fullness of Christian "salvation." We are saved *from* sin *for* a life of holiness. It must be both the negative of guilt relieved and the positive of holiness unleashed. Salvation is a breathing out (clearing the past) and a breathing in (launching the future).

Life in Christ should not be paralyzed in a pessimism mired in the assumption that persistent and disabling sin is inevitable for God's children this side of heaven. Instead, it should bristle with an optimism rooted in divine grace, an optimism flowering from belief in God's current presence and power. Rather than living in despair about present possibilities, a holy faith looks outward to the new, the hopeful, to the God who is active in the heart of the believer, and in the dynamics of the world even as it now is.

> Holiness defines the being of God. In turn, God wants us forgiven (exhaled) humans to share—inhale—the beauty of a cleansing holiness that enables us to be partakers of the divine nature—now. We are to actively and intentionally exercise the quest for holiness, the privilege of breathing deeply again.

Our *being* as well as our *standing* before God must change. Holiness is forgiveness of sin (standing) that also is supplemented with newness of life (being). We are to do more than exhale the old life. We are to inhale the new—*now*! Jeremiah's prophecy was about a new covenant that God would establish, one in which God would provide a *new heart.* Says God through Jeremiah: "I will put my law within them, and I will write it on their hearts; and I will be their God, and they shall be my people (Jer. 31:33).

No Pain, No Gain

The wrong timing choice says "no!" to the God who may be wishing to put a "yes!" on our humbled lips and fresh wind into our choking lungs. Holiness involves the full cycle of breathing. First is God's gracious breath of life coming our way; then comes the possibility of our exhaling our old selves through repentance and the inhaling of our new selves, our coming to share in the very life of God. This is dramatic and essential spiritual exercise.

Holiness defines the being of God. In turn, God wants us forgiven (exhaled) humans to share—inhale—the beauty of a cleansing holiness that enables us to be *partakers* of the divine nature—now. We are to actively and intentionally exercise the quest for holiness, the privilege of breathing deeply again. We must act on this pivotal fact. Christian faith is not merely about *knowing* the truth; it also is about being *transformed* by the truth. At stake are both our *sins* of yesterday and our very *characters* that are to be made new (Christ-like) because of the tomorrow that *already has begun in Jesus Christ*—and the today that can be changed because of the Spirit of Christ expanding our lungs and nourishing our lives.

True faith is about taking risks with God now, believing that God intends to make "new creatures" this side of heaven. No pain now, no gain now—or maybe even later. It is exercise time! The needed grace is freely available. God acts through gracious love; we then must react in grateful obedience. In his sermon "The Great Privilege of Those that are Born of God," John Wesley put the balance and responsibility of things this way:

> The life of God in the soul of a believer…immediately and necessarily implies the continual inspiration of God's Holy Spirit:

God's breathing into the soul, and the soul's breathing back what it first receives from God; a continual action of God upon the soul, the re-action of the soul upon God; an unceasing presence of God, the loving, pardoning God, manifested to the heart.... [But] God does not continue to act upon the soul unless the soul re-acts upon God.... He first loves us and manifests himself unto us.... He will not continue to breathe into our soul unless our soul breathes toward him again; unless our love, and prayer, and thanksgiving return to him.

That says it all. God first, new possibility of life, our needed reaction, and our resulting spiritual responsibility.

Get Off the Sidelines

What follows in these pages assumes that there are real Pentecost possibilities for humble believers who are willing to be deep wind-of-God breathers. These holiness possibilities are graciously and wonderfully true. In light of such truth, we will trace the essential rhythms of exhaling the deadening old and breathing in pulses of the new life, the holy life now possible in Christ by God's unmerited and yet amazingly available grace.

Holiness in this life may not fully duplicate what still lies beyond this world, a completed holiness beyond all present experience. Even so, it draws those of us who believe into the *present-ness* of the possibilities of our faith lives, highlighting what can and should be *on this side of eternity*. Whatever the eventual fullness of our spiritual lives that must wait until life beyond the grave, the important truth is that we are to be "going on to perfection" *now*!

Holiness is thought by many people to involve wearing funny clothes and getting lost in an unreal world of religious arrogance and deluded hypocrisy. Unfortunately, too many holiness people in the past have done things that have encouraging such perverted perceptions. Even so, true

Christian holiness will change a few things, causing some clash with the twisted cultures of this world. But it also will find ways to function constructively in the world, and will do so with an excitement, expectation, and pure joy not known by those who have never breathed in the fresh air of the Spirit of God.

Some of us Christians are still choking unnecessarily on the liquids of death! Our lungs are clogged and desperately needing to be cleared. We are still on the road to Emmaus, talking to Jesus without being sure who he is or what his resurrection is supposed to mean for us (Luke 24:13ff). We are holding the football in our hands when it is time to be passing it down the field, knowing by faith that the receiver is already on his way to the designated catch point. The rules of this faith game are all too clear. No throw, no catch. No pain, no gain. No exercise, no growth.

Staying with the football analogy, crossing that final line with the ball safely in hand is the point of all the rigorous training. Now it starts to happen! The runner has broken free and is straining every muscle to avoid the pursuing tackler. He is out in the open, and also out of breath, and yet breath keeps coming as the body rises to the scoring challenge. Flashing across his mind is the sign hanging in the locker room—"Get off the bench and into the game!"

Now the game is about to be won or lost as he runs with the ball, and the voice of Coach Jesus can be heard shouting from the sidelines—"Be perfect as your heavenly Father is perfect" (Matt. 5:48). "Keep running to the goal, breathing out and in. The Spirit is breathing with you, and even for you. You can make it!"

Holiness of heart and life is not easy or automatic, but it is God's intention for every member of today's church team. Here is the situation as described by Glenn Clark in his classic *The Soul's Sincere Desire*:

> Before it is possible to breathe, one must be surrounded by atmosphere, and the atmosphere must be *in one*. Likewise, before

it is possible to commune with God, which is a more conventional way of characterizing the deep breathing of the soul, one must know that God surrounds all and God is in all, that the kingdom of heaven is *here and now.*

It is! Therefore, pursue that holy breathing without which no one will see the Lord (Heb. 12:14). Go for the spiritual score. Go for it *now*!

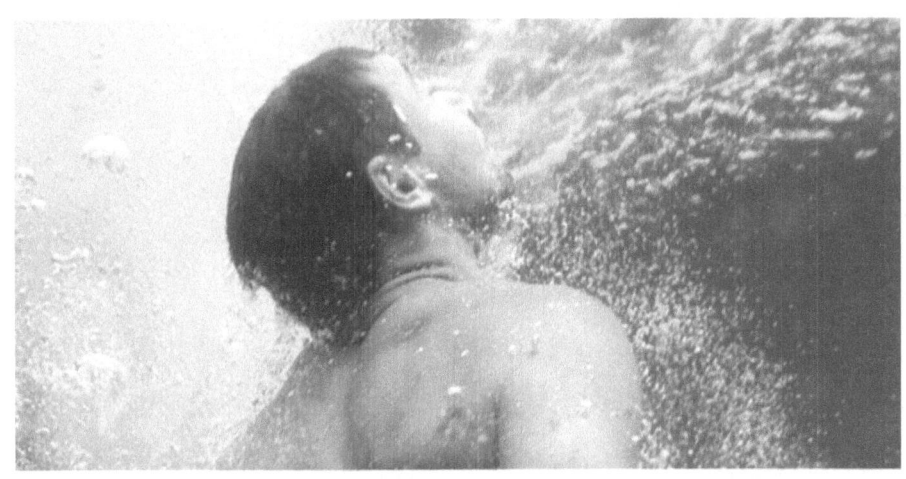

LETTING GO:
EXHALING

CHAPTER 2

FINDING THE RIGHT AGENDA

Lay aside every weight and the sin that clings so closely, and let us run with perseverance the race that is set before us... (Heb. 12:1).

To be holy is to be in the process of being formed by the Christ-like vision, practices, beliefs, and mission of the historic people of God. To be sanctified is to intentionally be on the way with Christ and in the midst of Christ's people, on the way to allowing the Spirit of God to re-form the image of Christ in individual hearts and in the community of believers.[6]

Here is where the current American society appears to be right now on matters of faith and personal transformation. It is a mixed and mostly breathless situation.

Many people with little or no church affiliation are nonetheless on a spiritual quest. They often are quite satisfied with putting together a patchwork of this and that, from one religious or philosophic tradition and another. They are happy to settle for feel-good "spiritual" experiences as long as there are few life-changing demands made on them. Opposed to the quotes above, they are hardly prepared to pay the price needed to "run with perseverance" and be re-formed in the "image of Christ."

Gaining the holy life really can happen before death, but not all at once and not without some disciplined effort (conscious breathing). The holy life is not a mere conforming to our church group's ideals or our culture's demands. It is nothing short of a conforming to Christ.

The consumer is king. A cafeteria-style spirituality is in vogue. Like on modern cruise ships, one wanders through a lavish display of food and takes whatever strikes one's fancy. Real personal transformation is rare because most people want the warmth of something "spiritual" with few belief requirements or ethical expectations attached, and often without any conscious relationship to God—after all, divine relationships can be demanding and isn't "God" just an old theory of the weak? In short, we have a spiritual marketplace "where many would like to be converted and justified, but few to be sanctified."[7]

The Right Breathing Program

The second quote heading this chapter brings to our attention a series of items that belong on the right spiritual agenda for serious Christians. They are in sharp contrast to the wide-open spiritual marketplace. To be holy, to receive, breathe, and exercise a truly Christian spirituality . . .

- Acknowledges the initiating grace of God
- Involves a conscious receiving of God's grace
- Means pursuing the goal of Christ-likeness now
- Is not merely a new or temporary religious fad

- Must include an actual re-forming of the heart
- Includes active life in the community of faith

In other words, a low-cost and no-strain "spirituality" is hardly enough. The right agenda for true Christian spirituality (holiness) necessarily includes the above six elements, and there are a few "nots" necessarily involved.

Gaining the holy life really can happen before death, but *not* all at once and *not* without some disciplined effort (conscious breathing). The holy life is *not* a mere conforming to our church group's ideals or our culture's demands. It is nothing short of a conforming *to Christ*. Holiness is a goal central to the biblical revelation about God's intent for us; it is *not* the contemporary fad of a few religious fanatics. Finally, holiness is *not* a solitary business, not just God and me. Holiness must happen in community and express itself in loving relevance to the needs around us. These several facts form a virtual definition of Christian holiness, and an agenda for its recovery in our time.

Holiness is a subject that fills the pages of the Bible and has deep roots in the church's history. In his 1950 *Requiem for a Nun*, William Faulkner writes one of his more famous lines: "The past is never dead. It's not even past." So it is with holiness. This vital subject has a long history in the faith of Christians and Jews before them, a history hoping to rush to the surface of the present, very much alive and still wanting to be received, breathed, and exercised to make possible a distinctive life for believers. Christian holiness necessarily involves the transformation of believers into truly new persons in Christ. The past of Jesus Christ is never dead and must not be allowed to be only the past. The future depends on it being *our present*.

Threads from Yesterday

Allow me to weave a few threads of this complex fabric of church history to make one basic point. Holiness is not merely a contemporary fad. It runs deep in the soul of the Christian community as a reoccurring urge to reform individual and church life into a more faithful conformity to the vision of the holy that is given by God's grace.

Our chosen few threads rise from an odd geographic fact. There are three expressions of this holy urge that all originated in the "old world" (Europe) and now are present as neighbors in rural Kentucky, USA.[8] Seeing these related bits of church history should be enough to make our point. There is nothing wrong with exercising our memories! What once was may indeed still be—or at least still should be. The past is not dead—it is not even past!

Holy expression #1. There was a Christian reform movement that began in 1664 in reaction to the relaxation of standards in many Christian monasteries in Europe. The resulting breakaway from the Cistercian order of the Roman Catholic Church was the formation of an independent monastic order called the Trappists, named after the La Trappe Abbey in France. Eventually, a group of Trappists found their way to Kentucky, establishing the Gethsemani monastery in 1848. A prominent twentieth-century Christian leader was Thomas Merton (Father Louis) who lived in Gethsemani for many years—and I, a Protestant, have done private spiritual retreats there over the years.

Holy expression #2. A "charismatic" religious group was formed in eighteenth-century England. The first members were known as "Shaking Quakers" because of the ecstatic nature of their worship services. They looked to women for leadership, particularly to Ann Lee. She called on her followers to confess their sins, give up all their worldly goods, and take up the cross of celibacy. Her small community was soon known for its enthusiastic singing, dancing, shaking, shouting, speaking with new tongues, and prophesying, all understood to be gifts of God known in the "primitive" church. By 1774, Ann Lee and a few of her "Shaker" followers had emigrated to America, with one branch soon reaching Kentucky, not far from Gethsemani.

Holy expression #3. John Wesley was another eighteenth-century Christian figure, a priest of the Church of England. He developed a passion for church reform focused around experiencing and living out Christian holiness. Some of his "Methodist" followers eventually migrated to the American colonies and soon became a powerful holiness force in the "New World." Asbury Theological Seminary, founded in 1923 in the little Kentucky town of Wilmore, now exists "to prepare theologically educated, sanctified, Spirit-filled men and women to evangelize and to spread scriptural holiness throughout the world through the love of Jesus Christ, in the power of the Holy Spirit, and to the glory of God the Father." Wilmore is not far from Gethsemani and the remains of the Shaker village.

These are three examples of the pervasiveness of holiness in church history, similar in impulse even if different in expressions. Two emerged in England and one in France, with all winding up as neighbors in rural Kentucky. While different, with the first two appearing rather extreme to most modern Christians, they and dozens of other Christian movements share a belief crucial for all modern Christians. Holiness should make a dramatic difference in lives and communities of serious believers.

The important difference holiness makes is seen in how Thomas Merton of the Kentucky monastery once characterized the neighboring Kentucky Shakers:

> They were simple, joyous, optimistic people whose joy was rooted in the fact that Christ *had* come, and that the basic Christian experience was the discovery of Christ living in us all *now* [holiness]: so that the true Christian is the one who lives and behaves as a "Child of the Resurrection" with his eyes open to a wholly

new vision of a redeemed cosmos in which war, hatred, tyranny, and greed had no place—a cosmos of creativity and worship.⁹

Many Christians over the centuries have sought to live as transformed children of the resurrection, just as the New Testament teaches and the Spirit promises. Their clothes, locations, times, and words often have differed, but their hearts, their in-depth breathing, have been much the same.

A Weight Problem

Our goal in these pages is to encourage all Christian believers to seek the wind of God and enter into the joys and disciplines of the holy life. Being Pentecost children of the resurrection is a significant and challenging calling. As we begin, an obvious question must be answered. Breathing properly? Is this a book about dieting, muscle building, and ancient Asian exercises? Is it a spiritual self-help manual? In some ways it is; in many ways it is not.

Am I going to claim that there are "holy" practices that will take off negative spiritual weight better than Weight Watchers or your local gym or the newest miracle pill? Am I going to argue that being a mature and growing Christian requires constant stretching and repetitive weight-lifting so that we can make ourselves into the powerful persons that God really wants? The answers are "no," and yet "yes," mostly "no," and yet necessarily "yes." Is that clear enough?

Make no mistake about one fundamental fact. Our being made new persons in Jesus Christ is God's work and not our manufacturing. The lungs may be ours, but the wind is God's. Nonetheless, God chooses to make us response-*able*, and thus *responsible* to cooperate with the gracious fact of God's wishing to be lovingly and transformingly active in our lives. God blows so that we can catch our breath.

All who come to believe in Jesus Christ continue to have a weight problem. The writer to the Hebrews says that we are called to "lay aside every weight and the sin that clings so closely" (Heb. 12:1). The right agenda for Christian living involves shedding the heavy weight of the old life, exhaling death, and assuming the lightness of the new, inhaling the Spirit.

I will refer to this laying aside of burdensome spiritual weight as appropriate spiritual exercise, the life rhythm of *letting go*, exhaling, and *letting God*, inhaling. Yes, the Christian life is God's doing. Even so, it also involves our intentional activating of various processes that encourage growth in the life that only God can give. The goal is the life of sin forgiven and new life received. The new is the holy life.

The basic facts are these. (1) We all have negative spiritual weight that needs shedding and holy strength and agility that need to be increased. (2) Progress in this shedding (exhaling) and strengthening (inhaling) will not come unless we are very intentional about proper spiritual breathing. The stakes are high indeed since we are talking about our human identities and destinies, our divine callings and responsibilities, and the very breath that it takes to live.

> *Why have there been so many passionate "holiness" reformers? They have kept appearing because many believers in every generation have allowed themselves to grow heavy and cold—not just old but dangerously breathless. There also has been a continuing tendency for the "establishment" church to add to the lives of the faithful the spiritually stifling weight of institutionalism, creedalism, and other "isms," often to the point of the faith itself being suffocated inside its own houses.*

If there is no positive progress at the spiritual level of our existence, we will be worse that overweight and weak; we will be stunted in life, never fully whole, never really happy, always immature, gasping for meaningful existence, and certainly not what God intends. Dare we even say that getting to heaven later may be in jeopardy if we do not engage now in holy breathing, if we do not *practice heaven here below*?

As we have said, attempts to address the spiritual overweight problem can be been seen across all of Christian church history. Why so many passionate "holiness" reformers? They have kept appearing because many believers in every generation have allowed themselves to grow heavy and cold—not just old but dangerously breathless. In addition, there has been a continuing tendency for the "establishment" church to add to the lives of the faithful the spiritually stifling weight of institutionalism, creedalism, and other "isms," often to the point of the faith itself being suffocated inside its own houses.

If spiritual life is rooted in God's free, unmerited grace, and it is, why must we engage in spiritual breathing exercises, almost as though salvation is *our* doing? The only adequate answer is a twin truth. First, because of the deep sin-driven disability we carry, we must *receive* before we can *respond*. Second, our receiving is ineffective in its grand goals unless we respond appropriately. God gives, and we receive; God blows, and we breathe; God makes possible, and we must choose to help make it happen.

Let's ask the important question again. Why act as if spiritual growth and health depend on us? Are we trying to earn our acceptance with God by dieting, stretching, and straining? Part of the answer is provided by Elton Trueblood: "Both the price and the glory of our finitude are indicated by the fact that *we do not arrive*; we are always on the way."[10] We must keep going. We are unfinished spiritual projects. But there is more to the problem we face than our finitude, our unfinishedness. Our sinfulness tries to keep us from even getting started in the right direction. Getting started properly must be God's doing.

To borrow the wise words of Paul to the Colossians: "So if you have been raised with Christ [God's doing], seek the things that are above" (Col. 3:1-2). The seeking is our part, our responsive doing. We cannot control the sunrise, but we can make sure that we are awake when it comes! We cannot create what only God's grace provides, but we are responsible to receive and nurture what God offers, keeping our life-doors open to the grace-gifts being made available. We can and must employ the vital exercise of seeking that which is from above, of breathing when the divine wind comes.

What, then, is the primary goal of the Christian life? Is it belonging to the right church, believing the right creed, or is it having one's character formed into the image of Jesus Christ? Is a real Christian one who is practicing for Heaven or participating in the divine life here on Earth—or are these the same thing? Is the real goal of our spiritual lives being fully "orthodox" in our beliefs and correct in our practices, or is it being *in right relationship with God*, knowing that we are loved and thus being liberated to love others? Understanding the meaning of Christian holiness grows out of proper answers to these questions. Answering them well forms the first items on the right spiritual agenda.

The quotation heading this chapter keynotes the particular understanding of holiness emphasized throughout this book. Specifically, it is the Spirit of God who re-forms us into the image of Christ. This re-formation is the heart of holiness. The Spirit works to newly caste our very characters. The renewing growth process necessarily involves our appropriate responding to God's expectations and enabling. Part of this process is a pattern of biblical practices and relationships, of breathing exercises and outcomes.

There must be appropriate Spirit-breathing practices if there are to be ideal spiritual results. And, yes, there must be some proper beliefs capable of supporting the practices. Holiness is a divine gift. However, if this amazing gift is not exercised, drawn inward with active breathing, and cared for properly, it will fail to flower as God intends.

CHAPTER 3

MOVING IN THE RIGHT WAY

> Jesus breathed on his disciples and said, "Receive the Holy Spirit" (John 20:22). Moving toward the gift of the Spirit is always movement in the right direction. It is being breathed on by Jesus himself.

> The church is a called people. The final goal is "a new heaven and a new earth," the kingdoms of this world becoming "the kingdom of our Lord and of his Messiah" (Rev. 11:15).... To play the role God intends in this great drama, we must be a holy people.[11]

All exercise involves intentional movement of some kind. Life is activity. A common wise saying is "use it or lose it." We must get moving. But some movements are good and some bad. Think before you act! Be aware that one prayer is the best movement of all. In classic hymn words:

> Holy Spirit, breathe on me
> Till I am all Thine alone,

Until my will is lost in Thine,
To live for Thee alone.[12]

If that sounds a little archaic, it's the language and not the meaning.

Words from a classic American play strike the important note. In Thornton Wilder's *Our Town*, Emily Gibbs dies while giving birth to a child and later is given the opportunity to relive one day of her life. She chooses her twelfth birthday and realizes in the awkward process of reliving her day how much every minute of life should be valued. She wonders whether anyone realizes the preciousness of life while they are living it.

Then comes this disturbing conclusion to her wondering: "The saints and poets, maybe—they do [realize] some." How sad. Most of us live our lives blindly, letting its richness slip by virtually unnoticed. We just sit there, doing nothing, hardly moving, drifting aimlessly, missing life itself!

Our spiritual lives in Jesus Christ are to be full, rich, and busily in motion. But so much of this potential goes unrealized. Wisdom and joy are found in the realm of the spiritual only when one comes to live deliberately and passionately in the glow of God's shared holiness. Does this sound like an abstract ideal far from where you live? It does for most of us. The desired glow is barely seen on a far-away horizon.

> *There are two basic rhythms required to be holy, the exhaling of death and the inhaling of life. Both must be intentional activities in order for a believer to be moving in the right spiritual direction—the direction that the wind of God is blowing. Spiritual growth toward holiness involves a conscious exhaling of the old life and an inhaling of the new life in Christ. Jesus breathes on his disciples and says, "Receive. Take in. Be filled."*

With that being the unfortunate situation, the question is how to get from here to there, how to set in motion some real progress toward that desired holiness, how to allow the divine glow to set us ablaze. Maybe holiness is a mere delusion, nothing more than a projection of our fondest hopes. But then—maybe not!

According to biblical revelation, holiness is no mere illusion. It is a gift from God that is real, but not automatically realized. Effective spiritual breathing is required and calls for deliberate movement. The problem is that some movements are helpful and others destructive. We must learn which is which, and then get moving in the good, the God direction. We must catch our breath—receive gladly the breathing of Jesus on us.

Speed Lines

Just like Emily Gibbs in the Wilder story, we allow so much of our lives to roar right past us. We travel so fast that we notice little around us, smelling none of the roses in our flurry of frantic activities. We are breathless in a dangerous way.

In one poet's imaginative eye there appears a biker. He is speeding, no helmet, head leaning forward, hair flying behind him in the wind. The poet imagines the trailing strands of hair as "speed lines," a symbol of what flutters behind as we rush along the roads of our lives.[13] We have been many places, and yet almost nowhere, not really. It is all a busy blur.

Our time of life is disappearing quickly—a reality we all must face. Rapid movement in some direction appears constant and inevitable. Given this, suggests our poet, we should look at things from the point of view of eternity. Whatever lies ahead, it is coming, and fast! Whatever our lives are supposed to be, they are constantly becoming that—or something else by default.

The speed lines are there whether we realize it or not. We have a choice, and it is a big one. We at least can choose the direction in which the speed lines fly. To be holy is to be headed home to God.

A Christian "saint," we suggest, is a believer who has chosen the right direction and is in proper motion, no matter the distance yet traveled (see chapter 5). We can pick the goal toward which we are moving, exercising in order to gather momentum in that God-ward direction. Again, movement is inevitable in life. To do nothing is to slide downward. Movement is good or bad depending on its direction. Sainthood is not reserved for the few successful spiritual arrivers. It is for those properly and purposefully on the right way.

This book is about life movements, intentional and ongoing movements. Unfortunately, we tend to wish that, whatever is wrong with us and whatever we need to do, there can be a quick fix. Let's do it and get it over with! But, in physical exercise or spiritual growth, it is not that simple, not that singular or quick. The life of faith is a journey, the ongoing search for wholeness in Christ—holiness.

We must decide. The decision is about setting the direction of our life's speed lines in a way that can enrich, liberate, and mature our spiritual lives—and in the process enrich those around us. We must begin breathing in the Spirit, taking deliberate actions, cooperating with God to become here on earth what one day we believe we can and will be more fully in heaven.

There are two basic rhythms required to be holy, the exhaling of death and the inhaling of life. Both must be intentional activities in order for a believer to be moving in the right spiritual direction—the direction that the wind of God is blowing. God's timing and our disciplined repetitions are required. Spiritual growth toward holiness involves conscious breathing out, resuscitation, exhaling the old life, and breathing in, inhaling the new life in Christ. Jesus breathes on his disciples and says, "Receive. Take in. Be filled."

Our current culture is pulling us hard in the wrong way. It encourages us to inhale commodities, not Christ, consuming everything someone else wants to sell. This is a spiritual capitalism that clogs us more and more and finally kills. Exhaling consumerism is an urgent necessity.

I ask you to do what I have done only partially most of my life. Please do not let the inadequacies of my past performance distract from what you—and I—ought to do now. I ask that we buck the trend of many preachers who have put the doctrine of holiness on the shelf because they are not sure of its biblical soundness or doubt their own ability to live such a sacred life in this world. In fact, holiness is biblical and God's grace is sufficient. Hear preacher Jesus: "Peace be with you [his disciples]. As the Father has sent me, so I send *you*.... He breathed on them and said, 'Receive the Holy Spirit'" (John 20:21-22). Holiness *is* possible, but only as one breathes in the *Holy* Spirit.

The fact is that true Christian holiness is not what many think. Holiness is *not* a large set of restrictive religious rules that are to be followed without fail. It is *not* the embarrassing pursuit of being better than others by flawlessly fulfilling God's intention for us, and in the process gaining the right to be judgmental of others of lesser flawlessness. It is *not* an impossible ideal to be delayed until some better world finally arrives.

So much for what holiness is not. Now to the positives. Holiness *is* the dynamic process of a growing personal relationship with a personal God. It *is* a journey, an adventure, a quest for Christ-likeness that never ceases because love cannot be exhausted. It *is* love, and God-like love is both a gift and a response, an enriching relationship and a disciplined life of faith and faithfulness. It is deeply breathing in the wind of God that then propels us forward.

Exercise and rhythm are essential to healthy life, physical and spiritual. If we want to grow plants, it will require our willingness to cultivate them regularly. Building muscle in our bodies requires the stress of many repetitions. Developing a rich and mature spiritual life also calls for disciplined intentionality. We must give regular attention to the inner life, cultivating its needs, exercising its muscles, and practicing the disciplines necessary to enhance one's relationship with God. We will discuss particular disciplines later.

As a senior American, I recently entered the world of Medicare and arranged for supplemental insurance. With it came a complimentary program called "Silver Sneakers." Aging people are invited to put on comfortable shoes, go to a participating health facility, and start exercising for enhanced and maybe extended life. I have checked it out, but have not done much about it yet—too busy, or maybe too lazy.

Yes, I am a little embarrassed. I admit that I have not done particularly well at focusing on what makes for health in the worlds of the body and the spirit. No matter about the past, however, yours or mine. I am determined to do better—and I invite, even urge, you to join in my determination. The goal is very important and there are proven ways for making progress. Some movements are good and some not. Just sitting where you are is definitely not good movement. Default leads to disease and eventually death.

Travel the Whole Salvation Road

What is the great spiritual goal? To put it simply and only somewhat misleadingly, it is to be "saved." This little word is a good one, although it says too little to most believers. It often says only that we need to be rescued from danger, saved from the awful judgment of sin, and diverted from a path that will land us in Hell. All of this is true, but is being saved only taking out fire insurance? It is that, of course, *and much more.*

"Salvation," being saved, includes learning who we should and can be apart from sin. It is actually becoming "holy" over time, and in this very world. It is to be "sanctified," set apart and made truly new in Christ by the Holy Spirit. We are both to be saved *from* sin and its consequences and then saved *for* something, a holy life in line with God's mission in this world.

"Salvation" should mean being rescued from all that is false and destructive and then being transformed into the fullness of the new being that God intends. As John Westerhoff once put it, "the spiritual life is everyday life lived in an ever-deepening and loving relationship to God and therefore to one's true or healthy self, all people, and the whole of creation."[14] This bigger picture of salvation will take some time and a lot of God's fresh air in our lungs. Even so, it is our calling and privilege.

For the Christian, this bigger salvation picture, this fullness of life is to become an actual part of the amazing story of God with us in Jesus Christ. To be "saved" is to be moving on the transforming road that is paved with God's grace. Conservative Christians have the reputation of being skilled at bringing people to the transforming road (evangelizing) and less successful at instructing them in traveling on the road toward increasing spiritual maturity. Getting to the road is one thing; actively traveling on the road is another.

The tragedy of life is not that eventually we all will die. It is that, prior to our deaths, what is supposed to be wonderfully alive in us never gets born! Being holy is moving on down the salvation road by being truly reborn, re-formed, re-engaged, re-related to a holy God in ways that begin to show in how we think and act.

I join a growing number of others in wanting to restore holiness to its rightful place of chief importance in the Christian life. The holy life, one fully surrendered to God, reflects a disciplined spiritual traveling, exercising that comes to show more and more the transforming power of God in and through our lives. Only actual transformation of life can be a convincing witness to the world and a means of unity in the church (John 17:11).[15] More impressive than "look how properly they believe" is this early public response to the community of the Christ— "look at how they love each other!"

Holy living is not monastic isolation or the path to religious pride and elitism. Rather, it is humble obedience to God, deep joy in the Lord, and mature faith that is sacrificially active in love. Echoing 2 Peter 1:4, we lowly humans are given an amazing invitation. We are invited to nothing less that a *participation in the divine nature*. As Howard Snyder puts it, we are called "to enter into the fellowship of Triune, self-giving love."[16]

Participation of this kind certainly will get attention and make an effective witness! The call to holiness is a call for the believer to put on traveling shoes and move on down the road paved by God's grace and patrolled all the way by the protecting and guiding Holy Spirit. Holiness is breathing in Jesus and then living out the life of the Spirit of Jesus.

Starting with God

The awareness of "holiness" is in some sense a universal experience for humans. The experience is that God works in *all people* for the potential good of all, with none having an excuse. There seems to be a power, a force, a reality outside our ordinary lives. It is mysterious, beyond full description, often frightening just because it is not well understood. This sense of *moreness* fosters in humans everywhere feelings of fascination, fear, curiosity, guilt, and excitement.[17] Prayer, for instance, is a universal phenomenon. At a minimum it is a reaching out of the self to something or someone greater than the self.

The related traditions of Judaism, Christianity, and Islam have named this living force, the subject to whom we pray, this ultimate reality, *God*. The "Yahweh" of biblical revelation is the Holy One who exists eternally, predates our reality, and is breaking into our histories with power, grace, and hope. The resulting call is for us humans to experience this awesome otherness and be transformed by exposure to it.

A beloved gospel song written by William (Bill) Gaither, a valued friend of mine, is titled "He Touched Me." Jesus once reached out his hand and touched a man who was reaching toward him in faith, and the man became clean (Matt. 8:3a). Being touched by the *Holy* One is to make us *holy* (Isaiah 6). Such touching is a gift in the present from the Architect of all time and meaning and life.

Holiness involves being touched and changed by the Holy One. Once touched, a person becomes set apart, becoming holy because of this relationship, no longer common or unclean. The Hebrew word for "holy" means "set apart." God has been touching humans: "the Lord your God has chosen you [Israel] out of all the peoples on earth to be his people, his treasured possession" (Deut. 7:6). This choice was not based on any special deserving of the chosen. Nor was it for their benefit alone. The people touched by selecting grace were intended to live for the eventual benefit of all persons on earth. God "did not call one nation *over against* all others, but called and formed a new nation *on behalf of* all others."[18]

What, then, is the beginning point of a proper understanding of holiness? It is none other than the nature of God who says that we are to be holy *because God is holy* (1 Peter 1:15). Obedience to this divine intention requires an understanding of God's holiness and then coming to see how that holiness might be received and shared through our believing and the surrendering our lives in faith.

True holiness will shatter the believer's resistance to the divine sovereignty that wants to reign in all of life. The biblical model is the original Exodus from Egypt

> *Central to the biblical witness is the proclamation that God is love. To be holy, then, is to love as God loves, loving ourselves, our neighbors, and the whole creation, and doing so vulnerably and sacrificially—just as God has done for us in Jesus Christ. We are to begin breathing in tune with the wind of the eternities. As we come to love like God, always enabled by God, we become a reflection of God's relational and Self-giving nature.*

that revealed God to be "majestic in holiness" (Ex. 15:11). This model became a pattern for the liberated people who were to share the divine character and will and to conform themselves to them in their own lives (Lev. 11:45). To be freed by the Holy One is to be free to become holy in his service. When God blows, waters part. We are to breath in that power and learn to really live with its momentum.

How is God holy? The essence of divine holiness lies in God's ways of relating. Much can be learned from the fact that God relates at all of creation. We learn from the Bible that God is open to and even affected by creation. The God who created has chosen, because of love, to grant to creation the dignity of being *co-creators*. This is amazing! The sovereign God is also the constantly interacting Lover of us all—and we are enabled to learn to love back. Central to the biblical witness, and thus to Christianity itself, is the proclamation that *God is love*. To be holy, then, is to love, to love as God loves, loving ourselves, our neighbors, and the whole creation, and doing so vulnerably and sacrificially—just as God has done for us in Jesus Christ.

Observing this defining reality of the holy God, we are called to *participate* in this interactive divine love. We are to begin breathing in tune with the wind of the eternities. As we come to love like God, always being enabled by God, we become a reflection of God's relational and Self-giving nature. We come to love each other and all of God's creation. We engage in what has been called "relational holiness,"[19] a moment-by-moment loving response to the nature and will of the ever-loving God.

Holiness is an adventure into the world of love. We are invited to carry a new passport issued by the holy nation that God is forming. Holiness is not to be a private and otherworldly experience, but active participation in a new society on the march with God for the redemption of a lost world. Holiness is the exercise of carrying, participating, and marching with brothers and sisters, the church. We breath new air and are part of the new-breathing family.

The source and example is God. The eternal being of God is a complex unity that lives in interactive harmony. We cannot explain this, only marvel at it. We call it the "Trinity," the three-in-one God who emerged in our human history as God in Jesus Christ. The guide for us now is the Spirit of this Christ who enables each step on our holiness journey. The Spirit allows us to participate in the love that flows among Father, Son, and Spirit. We are privileged to "receive the Spirit of God who gives the Son to the world. Thus we receive the dynamic outflow of the very life and love of the triune God."[20]

Joining the Conversation

A television interviewer once asked Dennis Kinlaw, "What is the most staggering thought you have ever found in your walk with God and your study of Scripture?" The Kinlaw answer was, "that the eternal God—who is Father, Son, and Holy Spirit—has invited me to enter into conversation with that exclusive group."[21] A wonderful answer!

What, then, is holiness? The best answer is not whether one smokes, drinks, gambles, uses drugs, is guilty of foul language, belongs to the wrong denomination, or baptizes with the wrong procedure. Being free of such things may well be marks of a holy person, but they are not where we should begin our definition. The best response is that of Kinlaw. We should begin with the staggering thought of having been addressed and invited by God into the divine life! We are privileged to breath with the wind of the eternities.

According to biblical revelation, we sinful humans have been invited to an ongoing conversation among Father, Son, and Spirit. We are asked to enter an intimate relationship with God's inner life (almost an unthinkable thought). Our faltering speech in such a setting is actually heard and taken seriously, and we are being asked to become "workers together with him" (2 Cor. 6:1 KJV). Says Kinlaw, "Our God so longs for us to be members of his own family that he makes us in his own likeness, allows us to know him personally, and counts us significant enough that he invites us to join him in his great work of redemption."[22] To know this, and to be in the process of becoming this, and to be busy implementing this, is to be *holy*.

What is holiness? It is the grateful acceptance of the divine invitation to serious conversation. It is activating by faith our divine gifts discovered during the conversation. We then are prepared to join God's work in this world as conscious extensions of the Father-Son-Spirit life. We are to be—and can be—living examples of the divine heart-cry of redeeming love. To be holy is to be intentionally in conversation with God and intentionally in the world on mission for God. It is exercising our intention to so *be* and so *do*.

Only when we know ourselves to be unconditionally loved by God can we be "holy," that is, can we accept this love and begin to love others unconditionally. Because divine love fulfills the law and true holiness is living the loving life of God, exercising holiness is not to engage in deadening legalism. We are not to be mechanical followers of a set of rules for absolute rightness. God's freeing and re-creating love is a law unto itself, a fulfilling of the older law (Rom. 13:10).

Having now laid a proper theological groundwork, we turn next to clues for quality breathing, guidelines that can help us on this holy journey. There will be some theology in what follows—a body without a skeleton is helpless and useless. But you can relax. There will be no struggling through swamps of theological abstractions. While you will see some doctrinal bones, our real concern is with the beating heart, the flow of life-sustaining blood, and the rhythm of exhaling our fallenness, and then inhaling the very life of God.

Be warned. The spiritual journey will not be quick and painless. No matter. Start by breathing deeply and slowly. Relax in the lap of grace. It is too important to worry about momentary distractions. It is time to start moving. Let's go on to holiness!

CHAPTER 4

GOING BACK IS MOVING FORWARD

It is when I am weak that I am strong (2 Cor. 12:10).

The breath of God entered them, and they stood on their feet, and those who saw them were terrified (Rev. 11:11).

Jesus makes it into a central axiom: the "last" really do have a head start in moving toward "first," and those who spend too much time trying to be "first" will never get there.
—Richard Rohr, *Falling Upward*

We said in the last chapter that movement is essential in physical and spiritual life, and that some movements are good and some bad. Now we ask, can moving backward be good? Are things like submission and humility positives in the spiritual life? Do we need to be weak in order to be strong (2 Cor. 12:10)? Do the last people really have a head start on eventually being first (Rohr above)? When God's breath enters his people, will they finally stand tall and be noticed by all—not because they have become divine bullies, not at all, but because they now are so wonderfully different (Rev. 11:11)? If so, God's kingdom is surely upside down in contrast to the world's usual thinking. Backing up can be really moving ahead.

Living in such a kingdom can be done only by catching the wind of God and beginning to breathe the very life of God. A precious friend of mine once put such catching and breathing into a responsive reading for worship settings:

> Leader: Catch the Wind!
> People: God, I'm so confused by all the noise, fragmentation, and busy bustle of my world.
> Leader: Catch the Wind!
> People: God, I'm scared. What if I can't cope with all that is demanded of me? Sometimes I feel like everything is caving in on me.
> Leader: Catch the Wind!
> People: It's not easy to be loving, to forgive those who hurt me so badly.
> Leader: Let the wind of My Spirit blow across your life.
> People: God, I want to be what You dream of my becoming.
> Leader: Trust Me, My child, and yield to the wind of My spirit.
> All: He is the Spring Wind—I am the grass. Let Him blow!

Holiness is new life found, real breath caught, fragile grass joyously dancing in the Spring Wind.

I Surrender All

When young, most of us participated in a little exercise in faith building. A couple of trusted friends would position themselves behind us as "catchers." We were instructed to stand with our backs to them, close our eyes, and fall backwards, trusting our friends to catch us before we hit the floor and hurt ourselves. It was a kind of falling upward, trusting the unseen to protect us when we became helpless. Falling back and being caught just in time is the way of faith. Giving ourselves away is the door to finding ourselves.

Spiritually speaking, trying hard to be first eventually will get us nowhere but last—hard words that most people do not believe. Life in the Holy Spirit allows us to know the amazing reality of being sons and daughters of God. In such knowledge, we become secure enough to respond to the call of Jesus to *insecurity*—"Follow me." But our anxious question is, where are you going, Lord? His only response remains, "Have faith and follow me. Catch my breath and trust. The rest is on my shoulders."

When I was a young adult, I often heard preachers call for yielding one's life radically to God. It was typical of the Holiness Movement of the late nineteenth century and beyond to announce things like: "Let go and let God"; "Surrender all"; "Come and put your all on the altar"; "Be soft clay in the Potter's hands." Yielding, going backward, giving one's all, these were the only ways forward and upward. These are critical spiritual exercises—yielding, letting go, giving up, and giving away, becoming breathless in order to really catch your breath.

I made reference above to a poem by Billy Collins about the long hair of a biker flying in the wind. Let me note another of his poems, this one called "No Time." The poet envisions a harried modern man rushing to work in the morning. The man drives past the cemetery where his parents are buried not far from the road. The driver is distracted momentarily, not by texting on his smart phone, but by imagining his father suddenly sitting up in his grave and looking disapprovingly at his all-too-modern son hurrying by.

With that discomforting look, reports the poet, comes a second movement that counters the first. The driver's mother also sits up from her adjacent grave. She tells her husband to lie back down and allow today to care for itself.[23] From at least the mother there seemed to come the wise word—have faith and let it go! Fall back, my dear, where you belong and just believe that the future will somehow be in good hands, now hands other than ours.

> *The essentials are (1) letting go—exhaling the old self and (2) letting God—inhaling the new self that God provides. Holiness is the journey from spiritual suffocation to a breath-full salvation.*

Parents have their roles in relation to children and a time to fulfill them as best they can. Life moves on, however, and the next generation must learn to take responsibility for itself. Life in general is that way. Early on, each of us deals with certain issues common to humans. Hard as it can be, when children become young adults the parents must let go. Then, hopefully, the new adults will get past elementary things and face well the larger issues of life.

The holiness tradition of Christianity has thought of the spiritual dimension of this progress as "going on to perfection." This going on involves the essentials of breathing, the dynamic of life itself. The essentials are (1) *letting go*—exhaling the old self and (2) *letting God*—inhaling the new self that God provides. Holiness is the journey from spiritual suffocation to breath-full salvation.

Stepping Double Time

There is a dual problem being faced. It is a doubleness at the heart of ourselves and our sinful condition. A single redemptive exercise often is not adequate to correct this complex problem. We are guilty persons and we are persons with gone-wrong natures. We *do* wrong because we *are* wrong.

Carl Jung speaks of the morning and evening times of life, each with its own "program." He says that one cannot live the afternoon of life according to the program of life's morning because what was great in the morning will be of little importance in the evening, and what in the morning was true will at evening have become a lie.[24] Put another way, there are two main tasks in our human lives. We are born and hope that someday we will find out *why*, the purpose beyond our mere being.

The first task of our lives is to build a sturdy container for life, a core personal identity; the second is to fill that container with what it was meant to hold. Transformation comes with positive movement from the first task to the second. Jesus spoke of the need for new wineskins to hold new wine (Mark 2:21-22).

Most people, unfortunately, get stuck in a preoccupation with the first task. They build their boundaries, identities, personal securities, and defense mechanisms. Then in their thirties and forties they begin living mostly inside their own walls and for their own selfish ends. They spend their adult years repairing and painting their personal containers. Building an ego identity is not altogether a bad thing, of course, probably even a necessary thing early in life. But the first task is only to be the first—not the only task. We are called to go on to something greater.

Be born, yes. But why? Build identity, yes. But always selfishly? Find ways to succeed, yes. But what about when the tasks are beyond our ability to accomplish, and selfish success becomes hollow, unsatisfying, and hurtful to others? Construct comfort zones for ourselves, yes, to a point. But what if spiritual maturity, wholeness, and holiness drive us outside our comfort zones? What if being weak is somehow the best way to be strong (2 Cor. 12:10) and choosing to be last out of a service motive is the right way to be first? Look again at the Rohr quote above and Mark 10:31.

The need is to do something very difficult. It is to transition from task one to task two. It is to take stock of meaning as well as security. It is to deal with the Jesus who kept bringing up the hard business of carrying a cross. It is being willing to stop breathing in supposed comfort in order to begin breathing in the more sacrificial air that offers eternal life. We finally must clarify our life intentions and somehow purify—have purified—our major motives. We must move from the selfishness of mere survival to the integrity of true being, being for others as well as for ourselves.

How do you know when you have moved from the first to a substantial dealing with the second spiritual task of life? You will know in part when "your concern is not so much to have *what you love* anymore, but to *love what you have*—right now. This is a monumental change from the first half of life."[25] It is when our concern as Christians shifts from *getting* in order to live well to *giving* as a loving way of living Christ's way. It is where we are more than satisfied to breathe with God's Spirit and go wherever that wind propels.

Protect ourselves, yes. We do live in a dangerous world, although guns, bank accounts, and insurance policies offer only limited and certainly not long-term protection. But what about loving and vulnerably giving ourselves away? A move from inward isolation to outward self-giving *is the holiness journey*. It can be frightening and not very inviting on the surface. Often, it will come only after some crisis or suffering, some shock to the supposed security we have created with our first life task.

The subject of suffering and the spiritual life will be considered in chapter 11. But first we must understand the double meaning of "sin" that makes necessary this second life task, this moving forward by finally falling backward. Sin has two realities, one an outgrowth of the other. Sin is *act* and *being*. It is what we do that is wrong, of course, but more deeply it is who we are out of which the wrongness comes. A glance at recent history makes this very clear.

From 1870 to 1914, the people of Europe tended to think that they were living in an era of peace, progress, and growing prosperity—the industrial revolution. But 1914 brought the terrible World War I. All the new progress had only increased the potential horror of the conflict. Soon to come would be another world war, with its atomic bombs—more technological progress being used for even greater destruction. The beloved humanitarian Albert Schweitzer lived through all of this, but refused to despair over the deep inclination of humans to destroy each other. Clearly the inclination is there. What is the solution according to Schweitzer? We must gain a true reverence for life, a reverence somehow no longer natural to us humans in our twisted condition.

Out of World War II came the classic novel *Night* by Elie Wiesel. He draws on his Jewish tradition that the Nazis tried to crush in the death camps. Wiesel portrays an evil that seems intrinsic in human nature, a nasty infection that we all have. Paul knew this infection. He spoke of it as "our old self" needing to be crucified with Christ so that "we might no longer be enslaved to sin" (Rom. 6:6). If sin is *act* and *being*, then we both sin and are enslaved to sin.

Any adequate solution must address both of these circumstances. First comes the divine forgiveness of our wrong acts, what we often call "justification" (relief from the penalty of our sinful actions). But that relief is not our full need, not the entire goal of salvation. More exhaling is needed. The goal goes beyond our history of wrong actions to the bigger goal of gaining the possibilities of Paul's grand announcement to the Roman church: "A new power is in operation. The Spirit of life in Christ, like a strong wind, has magnificently cleared the air, freeing you from a fated lifetime of brutal tyranny at the hands of sin and death" (Rom. 8:2, The Message).

The bigger goal? It is nothing short of becoming free of the "tyranny of sin," restoring our very being to the holy state in which it was created originally. That state is hardly an absolute sinlessness (a perfect performance), as though the holy ones are no longer finite humans. Rather, it is the presence of a pure love that can come to reign in the heart, a dominating disposition to do God's will and be God's person in this world. Acquiring this loving disposition is more a gift than an achievement, but even a gift requires exercise on our part—seeking, openness, breathing, willingness to develop the gift through discipline.

John Wesley's sermon "The Circumcision of the Heart" features the humility needed to acquire a new dominating disposition. After the penalty of sinful actions is resolved—forgiveness, justification—there must (can) come the deeper awareness of the gone-wrongness of our very beings. To be "sanctified," then, is to have removed the conceit of our own supposed perfections. In radical, child-like humility, we can receive the divine grace that enables a "habitual disposition of the soul" to the love of God. Holy love can come to reign in us by God's grace and our active willingness.

"Sin" is more than doing bad things. It also is choosing to stay on the surface of holy things, like the Bible and relationships to Christ and church life. The surface-only approach where most Christians live distracts from the real thing. It is like a numbing shot to the gums of the mouth that relieves pain without itself removing the rotten tooth causing the pain. It stunts a believing person. It is like playing with plastic animals and never petting a living dog or cat.

Bible reading, for instance, is a necessary Christian exercise. But it is not as easy as it sounds. Getting beyond the "plastic" surface of the words to the in-depth and contemporary meanings is a developed skill. The Bible needs to be approached in a relational way (prayerfully, obediently, in conversation with the church, in openness to God's Spirit). In fact, the Bible can only be understood "through the illumination of the Spirit who first inspired it."[26]

If reading the Bible, seriously and in depth, is an important but demanding spiritual exercise, so is eating.

Healthy Eating Habits

Holiness can be viewed helpfully in terms of healthy eating habits. Medical experts agree that keeping the body trim and healthy involves regular exercise, adequate rest, and a wise and disciplined diet. Spiritually speaking, one dimension of this discipline is *fasting*.

Jesus prescribed fasting and cautioned against its wrong use (Matt. 6:16). From a Christian point of view, it is not to be seen as depriving the body of what it needs, but rather a resting of the body so that it can best absorb what it already has and focus on more than constant intake and digestion. The other dimension of fasting—and this sounds contradictory—is *feasting*. It is the determination to eat more and more! Keep in mind that we are speaking spiritually, not encouraging the consuming of food until we cannot hold any more.

Jesus announced that he is the "Bread of Life" (John 6:35). He said that he came that we may "have life, and have it abundantly" (John 10:10). Why, then, do we not see in the church and in ourselves an overflowing of the abundant (holy) life? Might the answer be as simple as this? We have not feasted adequately on the Bread of Life or given ourselves completely to God in Christ. *Holiness requires adequate nourishment!* We eat too much worldly bread and fail to stop, fast, and feast on the Bread that is life itself. We need healthier eating habits—both fasting and feasting.

> *God's kingdom way of being is so upside down from the ordinary we see around us that we rarely recognize that it is actually the right side up, the way things can and should be. To be holy is to be healthy, normal, our original and intended selves.*

Advancement in the spiritual life is rooted in a growing humility. But advancing humbly runs against our many efforts to achieve, "get ahead." One poor exercise aimed at getting ahead is the *law-way*. One good exercise is stretching for the *grace-way*. It is difficult to accept the fact that going down may be the best (only?) way upward. Richard Rohr points out in *Falling Upward* that the idea of falling-down-to-rise-up is so counter-intuitive, so opposite to the mind-set of Western capitalism, so different from the assumption that our constant achievements will lead to constant growth and need fulfillment.

"Sanctification," entering and living the holy life, is the higher spiritual state that comes only by going down in humility in order to rise up in self-giving love. God's kingdom way of being is so upside down from the ordinary we see around us that we rarely recognize that it is actually the right side up, the way things can and should be. To be holy is to be healthy, normal, our original and intended selves.

Old phrases from the holiness tradition of camp meeting revivalism speak of this going down in various ways. People were called to kneel down at an altar, putting their all there, even coming and "dying to self" in order finally to be alive unto God. A song frequently sung during such altar calls was "I Surrender All." The call was to a humble falling down in order to find an amazing rising up.

Here is the really healthy eating habit. We must determine to allow God to help us exhale from a sinful heart the sin that destroys. Then we must begin to fill that vacated heart (eat of God's provision) by an inhaling of the Bread that is the very staff of life and yielding to the Spirit who is the power of life. We must catch God's (our) breath.

We can see in such fasting and feasting the essential rhythm of the spiritual life. G. K. Chesterton once said: "There are two ways to get enough: one is to continue to accumulate more and more. The other is to desire less." Should one choose the wisdom of the downwardness of desiring less, these words will be seen as compelling: To have what we want is riches, but to be able to do without is power. To do without, fasting, is a powerful path to becoming a new person truly filled with Christ, feasting, and lovingly propelled by the Spirit into world mission.

Far down—what a clever place for God to hide holiness! Recall that Jesus was born in Bethlehem, and not even in one of the better inns of that isolated little place. Only the humble and earnest will ever find God at work in this world, or their own intended place in that work. Jesus made clear that the first will be last (Mark 10:31). We finally must rise—by going downward. We advance in our spiritual lives by humbly opening ourselves to the inner building of a proper stable into which the lowly Christ will agree to be born.

I have spent decades in higher education as a student, professor, and dean. I am well aware of the danger of elitism in this setting, of people with impressive credentials or large titles who pull rank on others. It is all too rare to find the truly wise professor who has learned so much that she or he has become humbled by how little they really know. Moving to life in the church and thinking of the lowly Jesus in Bethlehem, "Most people get so preoccupied with their stable, and whether their stable is better than your stable, or whether their stable is the only 'one, holy, catholic, and apostolic' stable, that they never get to the birth of God in the soul."[27] Elitism is spiritual indigestion. It is the sin in our very being that is the opposite of holiness.

Early in life we inhale, gathering to ourselves what we think we need materially and spiritually to survive and get ahead. Later in life—hopefully—we exhale, releasing the old self that now is used up and no longer sustaining us well. As we let go of what once seemed necessary, we have opportunity to inhale anew. This time we receive by grace the very breath of God's living Spirit, the divine dynamic of the new self. While there will be a point when we decide to live on the higher plane of this new life (sanctification), we will continue to experience the exhale/inhale pattern of the old self out and the new self in (ongoing sanctification). Holiness is one-time and many-times, a crisis and a process. We are sanctified and we continue to be sanctified.

Spiritual growth is lifelong, a joyous, even if demanding, journey. It is never finished in this life and never runs on cruise control. Many religious people have a strong resistance to change, sometimes hiding their resistance under the cover of "being faithful to the truth." The hard fact is that, if change and growth are not deliberately programmed into one's spiritual life, faith usually winds up worshipping the status quo and protecting present ego positions to personal advantage—as if we had fully arrived, we were just right, we have all the answers. We sinful humans do not want to leave the comfort of a supposed superior "house" of assured faith for the unknowns of growth and change, even if it is Jesus who calls us on!

Maybe this is the meaning of that scandalous comment of Jesus found in Luke 14:26: "Whoever comes to me and does not hate father and mother, wife and children, brothers and sisters, yes, and even life itself, cannot be my disciple." This surely is not a divine call to violate the commandment to honor one's father and mother. No, it is a manifesto of our Master to give up all ego-rooted footholds and launch out with Jesus on a journey of faith that is fully surrendered to whatever God has in mind for us. It is a leaving of the houses we build for ourselves and a daring to occupy by faith whatever house God is building on our behalf.

CHAPTER 5

CAN WE BE "PERFECT"?

There remains, then, a Sabbath-rest for the people of God; for anyone who enters God's rest also rests from his own work, just as God did from his (Heb. 4:9-10, NIV).

We must distinguish between Christian perfection and "perfectionism."... Holiness is not the "second effort"; it is "the second rest." A believer who has yielded utterly to God and has received the infilling of the Holy Spirit is not uptight, trying to dot every *i* and cross every *t* in order to please God. [Instead], life is a perpetual Sabbath of worship, praise, and service in the Spirit of Jesus.[28]

Becoming new beings in Jesus Christ is the lofty goal and actual promise set forth for us in the New Testament. The word "perfection" often has been used to describe a truly new being in Christ. But that seems a very long reach. Perfection is a term that hardly can be applied to human experience and performance in this life.

All of us still-old creatures are so flawed! Sometimes we use the concepts of completion and perfection to describe our hope for ourselves, not our actual achievement. To use them for an already attained spiritual status and maturity is surely arrogance outrunning self-perception. Or is it? The answer depends on how we define words and on our trust in the sufficiency of God's transforming grace.

Credible Testimonies

The word "holiness" is typically thought of in the arena of super-saint, the rarest of believers among us. Charles Wesley, a great advocate for Christian holiness, admitted as much in 1762:

> If perfect I myself profess,
> My own profession I disprove;
> The purest saint that lives below
> Doth his own sanctity disclaim,
> The wisest own, I nothing know,
> The holiest cries, I nothing am![29]

This caution is well taken. Self-delusion and hypocrisy come to us so easily, unwelcome as they are. Even so, we must not be too quick to eliminate something that is really important.

John, the brother of Charles Wesley, used the word "perfect" in relation to Christian lives of love. He had reference to the substantial change possible from grace received from God. Such humble reception, he was convinced, leads not to haughty human claims of impossible achievement, but to an amazing, cleansing love available to Christian believers—even during their very-human lives in this very-troubled world. Christian perfection in John Wesley's view means to be cooperating with God's transforming grace, fulfilling Paul's instruction to "be imitators

CAN WE BE "PERFECT"?

of God, as beloved children, and *live in love*, as Christ loved us" (Eph. 5:1-2).

To be "entirely sanctified" is more about being *full* than *complete*. A person can be full of God's love and joy and yet be incomplete, still on the way, still in the making—as we always are in this life. When we are breathing the very wind of God, we are not God, to be sure, but we truly are God's redeemed and really alive children.

"Perfect" is an awkward word to use about mere humans. The apparent audacity of suggesting an attainable perfection in this life was addressed by John Wesley in his little book, *A Plain Account of Christian Perfection*. Recognizing well the danger of overstatement, he used more than half of the book to explain what he did *not* mean by perfection. The need for explanation was compounded when the Wesleyan revival of the eighteenth century in England came to the North American shores.

Once in America and now being called Methodism, this holiness revival movement soon filled the wilderness of the young nation with "camp meetings" and their frequent calls for the *immediately attainable* in spiritual life. Altars filled with people repenting, rejoicing, and claiming to be "saved and sanctified" on the spot. They testified to being forgiven and purified (perfected) in love by divine grace, all in the same week—or even in the same hour. The message and its reception were breathing in the air of the pioneer frontier. It was acquiring elements of emotion and the demand for

> To be "entirely sanctified" is more about being full than complete. A person can be full of God's love and joy and yet be incomplete, still on the way, still in the making—as we always are in this life. When we are breathing the very wind of God, we are not God, to be sure, but we truly are God's redeemed and really alive children.

immediate and comprehensive spiritual experience that were subtly changing the original message.

Could such instant-sanctification testimonies be credible, or were they only wonderful emotions somewhat out of control? Lives were changed, no doubt, and testimonies of God's work should be taken seriously and gratefully. Even so, often there emerged awkward things in the subsequent spiritual lives of these sincere believers now claiming to be "fully sanctified." They included new doubt and even more sin. Sometimes even more emerged. It was hypocrisy, something very unwanted and yet difficult to avoid as the need for additional spiritual transformation surfaced and seemed to conflict directly with the testimonies of "perfection" already claimed.

Consequently, we see today that even some "holiness" churches have backed away from emphasis on this teaching, now a little confused and embarrassed about excessive claims in the past. Some scholars in their ranks went back to the original teachings of John Wesley and determined that he had a balance on this subject that was easily lost in the dynamics of the American pioneer setting. Maybe it is time to back up, but not to an anti-holiness position. We should go back to the Wesley balance.

Both John Wesley and the New Testament insist on Christians opening themselves to the "perfecting" process. Discrimination is required, of course, but not a premature abandoning of God's promises and the potential of divine grace. Holiness is a biblical mandate and must be taken seriously. For Christians, holiness is a catching of our true spiritual breath, a going back to Pentecost and there finding the beginning to living out of the ruling presence of the holy God. We never "achieve" this by doing it ourselves, finally getting everything just right, thinking perfect thoughts and completing with full adequacy all of the proper actions. Holiness is a gift of the Spirit breathing with and through us.

There is an important paradox. It involves a recognition that there is *progression* in our *perfection,* always a going on from wherever we already are. Love is the core of the meaning of holiness as Jesus demonstrated it for us, and love can be full without being static. It can be mature and still in motion. It is a matter of what air we are now breathing, and whether death is being exhaled and God's pulsating life is being inhaled into our lungs of faith.

St. Francis fell in love with the poverty of God, the divine humbleness seen in the complete self-giving of Jesus. Richard Rohr, a Franciscan, takes from this that the Christian's spiritual goal is poverty (not some mechanical perfection). It is the humble releasing of ourselves, not the skilled achievement of perfect attitudes, thoughts, or behaviors. Kevin Mannoia pictures this well:

> Have you ever tried walking into the ocean or a river that is deep? There comes a point where you know it's over your head. You stand on your tip toes, desperately trying to keep control…. But there comes a point where you have to decide…to no longer trust the security of the dirt on the bottom or your ability to reach it. Rather, to trust the river. To honestly believe it will hold you up. It is a crisis point. A massive shift of confidence from your own ability to that of the river. From your own control to complete surrender.[30]

The big shift is from the place where our confidence lies to the direction of the energy flow. Mannoia concludes:

> The ongoing formation is not something that is merely up to us to achieve…. It's not simply a redoubled effort to exercise the spiritual disciplines so that we are spiritually fit…. Rather than try harder, becoming masterful [Master-full] is reversing the direction of energy. Not exerting our own energy to achieve, but releasing our grip on the selfishness that clogs our lives preventing the flow of God's Spirit from doing the natural work of

restoration. Agency shifts from us to God. The direction changes from our exertion to His appropriation.[31]

Note the breathing implications. Being actively holy, being full of the Master and alive in his love is more than a re-doubled effort at spiritual achieving. It is more than an intense working at certain disciplines, a maximum exerting of our available energy. Rather than our ultimate efforts to achieve, we are being called to allow a reversal of energy flow and to release our grip on the whole process. Back to Richard Rohr's point, we must commit to *poverty* of spirit rather than be focused on achieving perfection of performance. The goal is accepting the reign of love within which all law quietly finds its fulfillment.

To be holy as God is holy does *not* mean that we become all-knowing or all-powerful as God is. Nor does being filled with "perfect love" mean that we become flawless in our performance of God's will for us. It *does* mean that we have begun loving as God loves since the Spirit is putting God's oxygen in our lungs, God's love in our hearts, and is helping it flow through us to others. It *does* mean shifting confidence to the divine river of grace flowing our way and releasing the selfishness that clogs our lives and dams the flow of grace and power streaming from God to us.

Perfection Possibilities

There is wonderful news growing out of the amazing grace and clear desire of God. It is possible for us to be enabled in this life to imitate God's heart as we live in and show God's love. We can be "sanctified" as we become set apart to love as God loves. The New Testament presents this hope and expectation clearly: "God is love, and those who abide in love abide in God, and God abides in them. Love has been perfected among us in this: that we may have boldness on the day of judgment, because *as he is, so are we in this world*" (1 John 4:16b-17).

Christian perfection is no more and no less than the humble acceptance of the profound possibility of a new birth in Christ and then "Christ living in me." The right spiritual exercise is to catch our breath and reach for having Christ within, not worrying about getting everything right ourselves—which is impossible! Receiving the indwelling of the divine puts the impossible goal of spiritual perfection within reach since "it is no longer I who live, but it is Christ who lives in me" (Gal. 2:20). The goal of perfection gains meaning only because of the indwelling of Christ who enables our travelling the high and holy road of truly loving God and neighbor.

John Wesley often spoke against misconceptions of "perfect love" experienced in this life. Holiness is not merely avoiding evil, being morally clean in the public view, refusing to give any appearance of evil. As a boy, for instance, I was made to stay away from bowling alleys because smokers went there and people might think that I smoked too. Women wearing especially prominent facial make-up and/or jewelry were not allowed to be worship leaders or choir members because their appearance looked too much like "the world."

Are "perfect" Christians those who are so plain and placid that they are quite unattractive and bother no one? Hardly. Jesus certainly got himself noticed, not because he craved attention, but because his attitudes and actions rankled the social and religious status quo. Being *harmless* and *holy*

> Here is an important paradox. There is progression in our perfection, always a going on from wherever we already are. Love is the core of the meaning of holiness, and love can be full without being static. It can be mature and still in motion. It is a matter of what air we are now breathing, and whether death is being exhaled and God's pulsating life is being inhaled into our lungs of faith.

are not the same thing. Nor is holiness merely doing good. It is possible to be full of "good works" (which we should be!) and still fall short of the holiness without which we cannot even see God.

The concern should be to focus on *love* and resolve mis-readings of *perfect*—but without losing an important truth conveyed by using the word. Said Wesley:

> Hence I saw. . .the indispensable necessity of having "the mind which was in Christ," and of "walking as Christ also walked;" even of having, not some part only, but all the mind which was in Him; and of walking as He walked, not only in many or in most respects, but in all things.[32]

There is something profound, amazing, life-changing, "perfect" in view for Christian believers. Galatians 2:20 reminds us that God's purpose is that, in some divinely mysterious way, Christ may be *reincarnate* in our human flesh, living out the divine life of holiness in us!

The divine intention involves our being conformed to the image of God's Son (Rom. 8:29). Given God's goal for our re-creation, here is the critical paradox we must not miss. True aliveness in Christ, Christ's Spirit really alive in us, is an available spiritual experience that both comes in stages and yet can be "perfect" all the way once genuinely begun. Kenneth Jones said it well: "We may speak of 'perfect love' since love can be perfect without being *mature*. The love of a child can be perfect love though capable of years of maturing."[33] There is both a *point* of sanctification—when we yield ourselves fully to God—and a *process* of being sanctified when the full implications are worked out over time.

The New Testament word for "perfection" is a dynamic and functional rather than a static and technical word. While the Latin *perfectio* suggests an absolute without flaw, the Greek *telios* points to an intended purpose. A thing is perfect when it functions as intended. Perfect love is the substance of the law and the heart of the Christian gospel. The intended result is less a flawless performance of the divine will in this world and more a Christ-centered existence with a "habitual disposition" toward love, a holiness that is committed to the doing of God's will. Holiness is the reverse of an idolatrous self-love (sin).

Inhaling Divine Energy

According to an old text from the Orthodox tradition, we Christians are to adore God and receive "an influx of the divine." This influx reflects 2 Peter 1:4 where we learn that believers can be "partakers of the divine nature." "Partaking of" is the vision of Christian holiness. We actually can *share* in the life of Christ, *receive* the healing and empowering of divine energy, and *reflect* God's loving nature in our living. Here are three of the most important of all Christian spiritual exercises: share, receive, and reflect.

The phrase "divine energy" is crucial. It is important to be clear about this without getting lost in technical theological language. We need to learn about this from the great Christian traditions of Eastern Orthodoxy. The critical distinction is between the *essence* and the *energies* of God. The very being of God (essence) is never ours; what we can receive by God's grace is the flowing into our lives of the pulsating life of God (the divine energies). We become God-like, not God! We can be filled by God's Spirit without any confusion about our actually being God's Spirit.

Our being holy by God's grace does not violate these beloved words from verse three of the hymn "Holy, Holy, Holy":

> Only Thou art holy,
>
> There is none beside Thee,
>
> Perfect in power, in love and purity.

There, indeed, is only one God, perfect as we are not and will not be in this life. But, having said this, the good news is that God wants us and will help us to *participate* in the energies of his loving, holy nature.

The *essence* of God is all of God as God eternally is—one God, alone, in all of the divine perfections, ever beyond us mere humans. On the other hand, the *energies* of God are all of God as God acts, creates, loves, and redeems, re-creating the fallen in the divine likeness. Revelation is divine energy making the unknowable divine essence reachable and knowable for us, only partially of course, but enough to enable our salvation—our participation in God's loving and relating nature. We learn through revelation, especially in Jesus Christ, that God is love and desires and makes possible a *re-union* of Creator and creature in love.

Our sanctification means this. Through the reaching and redeeming energies of God's Spirit, we sinners can become participants in that energy, re-formed by that energy into its own likeness. By divine grace, we become like God without ever being part of God. We can truly reflect God's very being without being God ourselves. God's holy ones on earth radiate God's presence on earth without God ceasing to be God or his children ceasing to be true humans. Therefore, the call is to exercise our access to the divine energies and then "go on to perfection"!

The goal of the Christian walk of faith, the end of the holiness quest, is seen in the paradox of God's very being. Christians have come to know God through Jesus Christ as *Trinity*, three in one. We believe in one God who is at once Father, Son, and Spirit. This is a profound truth, not a mathematical trick. One plus one may be two, but with God it is one who, with nothing added, is also three!

There is within God's very essence a unity and a wonder-full diversity. God is both a *unity* of one and a *community* of three. God is love that is eternal and in action here and now. God is internally fulfilled and externally fulfilling. In plain language, we wayward and love-starved humans are invited to join the circle of love that God is prepared—even anxious—to share. Holiness is joining this circle, fulfilling the prayer of Jesus that "they may all be one." Prays Jesus, "As you, Father, are in me and I am in you, may they also be in us, so that the world may believe that you have sent me" (John 17:21).

The receiving, reflecting, and sharing of the divine love energies are at the very heart of Christianity itself. They are three critical exercises for Christian health and integrity. Holiness is the paradox of a falling upward, the descent of God to our human plane in Christ so that we sinful humans might rise to a reuniting relationship with God through Christ. First, God exercises, projecting into creation the love that God is eternally. Then we have the grand opportunity of exercising faith and receiving into ourselves the love being projected our way. We love because God first loved us!

Moses encountered God in the burning bush and then became "like God to Pharaoh" (Ex. 7:1). According to the New Testament, "we are children of God" (1 John 3:2). We are not God, but by sheer grace we can become able to share in God's very life, being like God, witnessing faithfully to the pharaohs of this world. As God's children, we come to share characteristics of the Father. We are transformed into the likeness of Christ in order that we might be examples and agents of his glory and healing power.

Daring to Be "Saints"

Please hear this—and then dare to act on it. Holiness is *not* an abstract and unrealistic vision; it is at the center of what God is all about with us. Christ is to reign within us so much so that we become conformed to his very image. We become transformed into the divine likeness through God's life-giving Spirit (2 Cor. 3:18). We become "saints" of the Most High.

The numerous biblical references to the Spirit of God come down to two experiences: God-at-hand, *intimacy*, and God-at-work, *potency*. The intimacies draw us in, renew our breathing, and the potency thrusts us out, allowing God's wind to blow through us. We are loved and then we love. God comes and then, *together*, we can go on mission. To be a saint is to be a fellow-traveler with the God who is present and on the move.

Here is a great paradox, both aspects of which are true and necessary. On the one hand, we sinners are responsible to partner with God in the growth of our spiritual lives. Growth requires our consciously breathing and regularly exercising. On the other hand, holiness is God's agenda for us—and it can be empowered *only* by God's enabling grace. We can be saints encouraged because of God's will and grace working for our true transformation. We must remain necessarily humble but *not passive* about our own supporting efforts. The sovereign God acts first, freely, lovingly. Then, because of and enabled by God's actions, we can and must respond, repent, receive, and determine to grow through spiritual exercises designed by God for just such a marvelous purpose.

When are we Christians "perfect"? When we are fulfilling the purpose for which we were created. God's creative purpose was a world of relaxed, beautiful, self-giving, interactive love and lovers, as when God walked in joy with Adam and Eve in the garden, unhindered by sin. Who, then, are the "saints"? They are "those who develop a lifestyle of love [and] stand as poignant witnesses to grace at work in the world. These virtuous ones also enjoy the benefits of abundant life that love brings."[34] They are again garden walkers with God.

The holy ones are "adult" Christian believers. However, we should not measure holiness by years old or time in the faith. Spiritual growth continues before and after the initial experience of "Christian perfection." How then do we identify the *point of attainment*, the time of being "sanctified" while yet going on to "perfection"? It is at the point when the humble, gentle, and patient love of God and our neighbor begins to rule our "tempers, words, and actions."[35] It is when divine love has both *entered* and has begun *ruling* in our lives of faith.

CAN WE BE "PERFECT"?

This setting apart unto holiness by God's grace involves both God's initiative and our willing response and disciplined participation. Holiness is a moment-by-moment growing reality and pursued challenge, clearly a gift and yet also a learned way of living and going on. It is gladly received and daily developed.[36] It is *separation* for sure, but separation of a special kind and to a particular purpose.

Holiness is being separated from evil, being set apart "from the world." But, since Christian holiness is a life of love, it involves *difference* without *distance*. We are no longer to be *of* the world, part of the evil, but still *in* the world so that God can love it and redeem it through us. Being like God is loving like God—relating redemptively like God.

A "saint" is hardly a Christian who has reached the fully developed spiritual state where ignorance has evaporated and attitudes and behaviors have become precisely what they ought to be. Instead, a saint, a holy person is the Christian who has been truly "converted" or turned around by God's forgiving grace and then has chosen to begin exercising in order to build momentum *in the right direction*. A critical Christian exercise is *turning around* (conversion). Another is getting into God's gear and moving on down the road of love.

> *The numerous biblical references to the Spirit of God come down to two experiences: God-at-hand, intimacy, and God-at-work, potency. The intimacies draw us in, renew our breathing, and the potency thrusts us out, allowing God's wind to blow through us. We are loved and then we love.*

While the turn of conversion must never be minimized, the saint knows that it has to be intensified. Holiness is the intentional quest of the believer to be a complete and active "yes" to God in love. The saint is the one who has ended the "I" protection and projection. The "I" has come into conscious union with the "I AM" of God. Such union overrides any need for self-hatred or self-rejection. There is no need to be perfectly right—that is not possible or necessary anyway. The task is to be in genuinely *right relationship* with God's Spirit and God's mission and manner of life. To be *holy* is to be *whole* in relationship with God through Jesus Christ by the power of the Spirit.

The "saintly" spiritual life is the emergence of healthy, self-critical thinking that allows one to see beyond the shadows and disguises of the sinful life and find one's true identity as being "hidden with Christ in God" (Col. 3:3). Saints are those joined to Jesus closely enough to share his mind (Phil. 2:5-11). The very character of a saint is being reshaped by Jesus through the exercise of clinging to him by the grace and power of his Spirit.

Christ Formed in You

The Apostle Paul wrote to the troubled believers in Galatia: "My little children, for whom I am again in the pain of childbirth until *Christ is formed in you*" (Gal. 4:19). The goal of the Christian life involves two critical exercises, two phases of complete "conversion." One is to *turn* toward Christ, repenting and being forgiven; the other is to consciously commit to and actually *walk* in that new way with Christ in this world. Paul urges believers who have turned to now walk worthy of their calling (Eph. 4:1). This "walk" image means the proper and daily ordering of one's whole life around the reign of God's love.

Holiness, wisdom in the Hebrew sense, is "bringing all of the dynamics of your being into harmony with the word [that] God is speaking you forth to be in the world."[37] Have you been forgiven, your yesterdays cleansed by God's grace? If so, now dare to be God's saint, a Christ-formed word being sent to the world. Bring your life into the presence of God's sanctifying presence. His transforming power can make possible a "perfection in love" because "God's love has been poured into our hearts through the Holy Spirit" (Rom. 5:5).

CAN WE BE "PERFECT"?

In this way, we are increasingly re-created by the Spirit to be like Jesus and set apart by God for a holy life. Our love-less fallen nature (sin) is cleansed into a righted relationship with God and all our neighbors. When we do come to live in a truly loving relation to God and others, we are perfect

> in the sense that we are being what we are created to be. We are perfect in intention, for the underlying motivation of our lives will be to love God and neighbor. We are also perfect in direction, for our lives will be aimed toward becoming increasingly Christlike...increasingly a person of love. This is the sanctified life, the life set apart for loving God and others.[38]

The deeper Christian life has been covered too long with a thick layer of emotionally charged and misunderstood words—like "perfection."

Are you confused by the meanings and purposes of perfection, baptism with the Spirit, sanctification, predestination, saint, etc.? Have you seen these words used as clubs on fellow believers rather than precious invitations to their true fulfillment? Some clubs bring a nasty ringing in the ears. "You must...or you are second-class believers who do not fit with us." "Agree or be gone!" Heed this wise advice:

> The question you must ask yourself is this: am I alive unto God? [H]ave I experienced the fruit of my conversion? [D]o I have an anointing from God? [D]o I really love the Lord and his Word? If you are unsure, then stop arguing over terms and start yielding your life to God so that he may fill you with his Spirit.[39]

Is there a fire in your spiritual fireplace? Is there really life in your living? Whose breath is filling your spiritual lungs? Is the Spirit in the center of who you are? Or are you stuck with resisting religious rules and expectations that seem to care more about themselves than your well being?

Do you resist spiritual discipline because you fear it will be restrictive and deadening? Please know this. The Christ-walk is about *life*. Start breathing!

"Perfection" was a prominent theme in John Wesley's life and teaching. He saw its pursuit as opening and not closing life. Such a full and disciplined spiritual life was not thought burdensome, but liberating. It was "not a morbid affair under an unbearable burden of guilt going on to a destructive self-examination and condemnation. Going on to perfection was a way of living that offered freedom, meaning, and joy. To be moving toward perfection was to be moving toward life at its best."[40]

Christian perfection is a second "stage" or phase in spiritual development (even though the whole process is dynamic). It is a second childhood world where things again are "enchanted," but now not with imaginary friends, but with the amazing wonder and mystery of God's Spirit. It is an "in-Spirited" existence, a matured childhood chastened by all the complexity and pain of life without being deadened and disillusioned by them. It is the simple happiness of childhood again, but not with eyes closed in unawareness or denial, but wide open to see much more than the crowd of faith-less people are prepared to see.

The spiritual second childhood is a perfected wisdom that is learning to live comfortably with mystery, doubt, paradox, and "unknowing." Being perfected in love is to have *arrived* while yet *being on the way*. This description may not be rationally "clean" to the scientific mind, but it can be experientially rich to the Christian pilgrim yielded to the life of love. We are no longer to be the uninitiated kind of children who are easily tossed about by every wind that blows (Eph. 4:14). We are, however, "to receive the kingdom of God as a little child" (Mark 10:15). It is only to such "that the kingdom of God belongs" (Mark 10:14).

What about sainthood being understood as a reduction to childhood? This is hardly the world's way, but it is *the* way to catch your breath and really live again. So, let us be spiritual children, loving little ones who are full of faith. Let us be children who are not hesitant to move on, questions and all, and who are not afraid of sainthood, human limitations and all. We see several times in 1 John the designation of believers as "little children," and we recall that Jesus said, "Unless you change and become like children, you will never enter the kingdom of heaven" (Matt. 18:3).

Be Not Anxious!

John Wesley's focus on holiness was expressed in a variety of ways. In addition to speaking about holiness in terms of love for God and neighbor, he also spoke of it in terms of joy, happiness, thankfulness, prayer without ceasing, purity, obedience, fruits of the Spirit, and doing all to the glory of God. As such, holiness represents both a gift and a task. As a gift, God grants righteousness to believers by saving grace through the work of Jesus Christ. As task, God enlists those same believers to respond in faith, hope, and love to the offer of sanctifying grace.

> *Is there a fire in your spiritual fireplace? Is there really life in your living? Whose breath is filling your spiritual lungs? Is the Spirit in the center of who you are? The Christ-walk is about life. Start breathing!*

Being *set free* is to be supplemented with being *set apart*. God initiates, nourishes, and completes the sanctifying process. Yet, paradoxically, God requires our response and what is complete continues to evolve. We catch our breath and then we keep breathing, moving on in faith instead of with anxiety.

Wesley thought that believers should seek to experience Christian perfection, or entire sanctification, words describing a deepened and advanced Christian life. Sometimes conceived as a "second work of grace" subsequent to conversion, he thought Christians should live a more holy life, enabled by the sanctifying work of the Holy Spirit in their lives. Such a life should manifest holy thoughts, words, and actions, and a holy resting in the adequacy of God. Wesley was optimistic about how much the sovereign God of the universe might transform believers into holy examples of Christ-like being and living.

These days we might choose to think of Wesley's concept of holiness as *wholeness*. The holistic pursuit of personhood represents the kind of holy healing that God wants to perform in our lives. This need for holy healing of our deepest wounds accounts for the prominence of therapeutic language in Wesley's various comments on human salvation. Indeed, Wesley characterized the very essence of religion as a *therapeia*—therapy by which the Great Physician heals our sin-diseased souls, restoring the vitality of our lives.

Two things are incompatible: trust and worry. To worry is to admit that trust has failed. What is the source of real trust? There must be a sense of love-inspired wholeness at the core of our being that warms the depths of our most frozen fears. This wholeness surely comes from acting on these classic words from the Anglican *Book of Common Prayer*: "O God! Who is able and willing to assist me, what grounds have I not to place my whole confidence in you, to throw myself into the arms of your providence, and wait the effects of your bounty?"

The world tends to gather possessions as insurance against anxiety. Big bank accounts mean few fears, or so foolish people think. We have seen repeatedly that such an assumption is nonsense. Dietrich Bonheoffer was clear: "Be not anxious! Earthly possessions dazzle our eyes and delude us into thinking that they can provide security and freedom from anxiety. Yet all the time they are the very source of all anxiety."[41]

By contrast, the believer who hopes to "go on to perfection" proceeds in trust that God's sanctifying and sustaining grace is available and adequate. Before her death from cancer, a good friend of mind published *Steady Till Sunset*.[42] Near her life's end and at the end of this book about her "incredible cancer journey" she writes: "Always. Forever. No matter what CT scans and blood tests show and doctors proclaim. No matter how I feel. No matter what. None of these change or challenge the always faithful, always powerful, always in control God." Be holy—and not anxious!

CHAPTER 6

BUT NOT SO FAST!

Stay here in the city until you have been clothed with power from on high (Luke 24:49).

Thus says the Lord God to these bones: I will cause breath to enter you, and you shall live (Ezek. 37:5).

You insist upon it, that we are saved by faith: And, undoubtedly, so we are. But consider, meantime, that let us have ever so much faith, and be our faith ever so strong, it will never save us from hell, unless it now save us from all unholy tempers, from pride, passion, impatience; from all arrogance of spirit, all haughtiness and overbearing; from wrath, anger, bitterness; from discontent, murmuring, fretfulness, peevishness.
—John Wesley, in his sermon "On Charity."

A runner does not go straight to the starting line before first dressing properly and stretching muscles that suddenly will be relied on heavily. Go and do for Jesus, of course, but first stay in the city and be clothed with his Spirit. This staying and being clothed is so necessary before the activities of the Christian life begin and its challenges are faced (Luke 24:49). We are instructed to wait and be encouraged that fresh breath will come to bring new life.

Speed is a great asset in many sports and exercises. Do it fast and you tend to win. Not so, however, in the Christian life. We cannot use shortcuts, rush through growth tasks, and mindlessly speed our way toward heaven. We must slow down and deal with some crucial realities in the present. The Christian spiritual life is not a race, especially not at first. We have to slow down, cherish and nourish the journey, and sometimes deal patiently with things like persistent "unholy tempers" (see Wesley above). We first need to catch our breath and benefit from the breathing of the Spirit for whom we wait.

Many believers in Jesus, thrilled by the Spirit's initial presence and power, are in too much of a hurry. They start gulping air and become almost breathless again. They say, "If holiness is the wonderful and possible goal of Christian life, let's get to it right away!" But a paced breathing is involved. Accomplishing all that John Wesley suggests in the quote above cannot happen by thinking that we can rush down a spiritual sports field for a quick score without a carefully planned play and the skill of dedicated teammates.

Older persons who have not exercised much for a long time are tempted to vigorously test out their muscles on special occasions. Maybe it is a snowfall that needs shoveled off the driveway as soon as possible. An older man gets out of his rocking chair and starts out full speed, like when he was a teenager, and quickly gets into trouble. Unused muscles strain to keep up and easily get torn. The older heart suddenly loses its normal rhythm. Breath becomes frantic. Then the lights go out and it's ambulance time.

Too much all at once may be worse than nothing at all. Likewise, deciding to be a mature Christian at a moment's notice usually leads to frustration and a crippling hypocrisy. The ripening of apples, oranges, and human hearts has its own timing. We are dealing with the complexity of attitudes and relationships. So, not too fast!

Resting Is Good Exercise

Here is how Tuesday became the traditional voting day in the United States. A long time ago the country was very religious and primarily rural. Wednesday was a busy market day. Sunday was the day of worship, while Monday could be used to travel by buggy to the voting centers after a weekend of rest and worship. So, Tuesday was the day that worked best for most people wanting to vote. Now society is so different. Nearly all people are close to voting centers and cars are widely available. Even so, Tuesday remains the voting day—tradition.

Civic and spiritual life are similar in many ways. Whatever the day of the week, what matters most is the willingness to slow down and register our political opinions and address the internal issues of our private lives. So many of us, now potentially available on any day, find voting or praying inconvenient, not important enough to get on our crowded schedules. Democracy can be a risky business when people are overloaded with other priorities and many fail to participate at all in political life—except by occasionally complaining. Likewise, Christianity can be at risk when believers fail to exercise as they should their God-given rights and responsibilities.

> *Many believers in Jesus, thrilled by the Spirit's initial presence and power, are in too much of a hurry. They start gulping air and become almost breathless again. They say, "If holiness is the wonderful and possible goal of the Christian life, let's get to it right away!" But a paced breathing is involved.*

The violin virtuoso Joshua Bell agreed to a social experiment organized in 2007 by the *Washington Post* and then reported in that prominent newspaper. Soon after performing in Boston's Symphony Hall where tickets began at $100 each, Bell took his $3.5 million Stradivarius to a metro train station in Washington, D.C. Dressed in an old T-shirt and baseball cap, he played masterpieces of classical music for the commuter crowds that rushed past him. A few at least hesitated and then tossed a bit of money into his kettle; most hardly noticed and hurried on past a completely free, world-class concert.

The questions are obvious. Is any day of the week now too busy for us? Has our awareness of the greatest of all been deafened by our rush to get somewhere or do something else? Have the games on our smart phones and the music plugged into our ears cut us off from the people and events within arm's length? Is the Christ of God sitting quietly on our routes, right by our sides, almost being stepped on and yet politely ignored? Rather than his kettle asking for donations, Jesus is carrying an unnoticed sign that reads, "Given freely for you." Very few of us notice anymore.

Holiness requires our choosing to slow down, reading the sign being carried by Christ, making ourselves fully available to the loving stranger in the station. We must begin to live face-to-face with and full of the love of this Savior. Holiness is the quietness, stillness, and richness of Master-full living. Such living generates a wholeness that integrates who we are inside with what we do outside. Being Master-full is not a matter of setting an extra-high set of standards, imposing an enhanced range of admirable behaviors that now are possible to achieve because of a honed set of spiritual performance skills. Holiness is not doing more and more, faster and faster, and hopefully better and better. It is slowing down long enough to enter into the source of life—being filled with and re-formed by the breath of the Spirit of life.

The mature Christian faith involves high standards and particular behaviors, of course. But reaching and enacting them comes less from following perfectly what we think is the supreme rule-book of God and more from an increased yielding to the grace-full Master, being filled with his love, and permitting that love to flow from God through us to others. The issue is more grace than "works," more relationship than rules. Although risky to say, it is even more than the "right religion."

A dear saint of my acquaintance was crossing the Pacific Ocean on a slow freighter, returning to her missionary assignment in Japan. After days of building a relationship with a fellow passenger, a crude businessman, she realized that he was spiritually hungry and had come to respect her. One day he said to her, "Ann, if I got saved by your Jesus, would I have to stop smoking?" Her wise response was, "First, get better acquainted with Jesus and then you can ask him." He had expected a clear, "You sure will!" Instead came the gentle invitation to go slow and do first things first.

There is an important fact to remember. In the earliest years of the Christian church, the Holy Spirit was an *experience* more than a *doctrine* or a developed code of right actions. The church was a living fellowship and not yet a set of institutions with fixed leadership offices and detailed creeds. The mission life of the church began with a "Not so fast!" The disciples of Jesus were thrilled by the resurrection news about Jesus and would not be silenced. But the resurrected Lord instructed them *to wait* (Luke 24:49). Believers must breathe in and *taste* as well as hear the good news of God. They must enjoy a leisurely meal with Jesus. Having encountered the Christ, those first disciples had to ingest his Spirit, allowing the encounter to become central to who they were.

> *In the earliest years of the Christian church, the Holy Spirit was an experience more than a doctrine or a developed code of right actions. The church was a living fellowship and not yet a set of institutions with fixed leadership offices and detailed creeds.*

We still must go into all the world, but how? By propelling ourselves with great planning, fundraising, and church programming? Yes, partly, but no, not mostly. We are to go by gliding patiently and humbly on the wind of the Spirit!

Jews had known this spiritual truth for centuries. The prophet Isaiah once said that "those who wait for the Lord shall renew their strength, they shall mount up with wings like eagles, they shall run and not be weary, they shall walk and not faint" (Isaiah 40:31). The psalmist echoed, "For God alone my soul waits in silence; from him comes my salvation" (Psalm 62:1). The Christian's program of spiritual breathing and exercising should not begin in a flurry of activity. We must wait, taste, come to know inwardly, transformingly, that God is loving grace that is meant just for us!

Why not so fast? A carefully placed beginning is necessary because we must be changed ourselves before we are ready to set out to change others. Credible witnesses to the risen Christ must be free of guilt for their sinful pasts *and* somehow made new persons whose lives have come to match their words. We are to be touched and filled with the Spirit. We must be empowered to be witnesses to our resurrected Lord (Acts 1:5, 1:8, 2:1-4). Again, sin is both wrong *acts* and wrong *being*. Full awareness of and dealing with the *being* part rarely comes with the initial experience of forgiveness of past acts. Wait—be forgiven *and filled*—then go!

Usually, in order to move on from forgiveness to spiritual depth and maturity, it is necessary as a new believer to face a few personal failures and some form of suffering. These make one keenly aware of the depth of the sin problem—and thus the additional dimension of its available solution by God's sanctifying grace. On this spiritual journey, there rarely is a non-stop flight on the schedule. As Jesus once put it, you must come to recognize the big plank in your own eye. Only then will you see clearly enough to take the little splinter out of the eye of another (Matt. 7:5). Witnesses to Jesus will hardly be credible when pointing out the needed repentance of others while a little log of hypocrisy is hanging out of their own eyes.

Growth takes time, patience, holding still, even being purposefully passive while learning to enjoy the sounds of silence in God's presence. There should be a plan for prayerful quietness. Prayer is not constant talking toward God in a special religious language; it should be more an intentional listening for God's responding voice. True listening and true spiritual maturity involve a releasing, a letting go and letting God. A point of holy communion with God can be reached where words fail to be adequate and are no longer even necessary. After all, our skill at manipulating words means little to God, who prefers to read and change the heart, or as Wesley puts it above, save us from "unholy tempers" and much more.

Being intentional about breathing in the Spirit can reach a point of intimate spiritual relationship with a hearing and loving God. At that point, "the only reasonable action is that of yielding oneself to the experience."[43] Our most appropriate response is to stop the flow of our words and ponder the pregnant silence, to risk ceasing our efforts and opening to God's energies. The call is to set aside our agendas and be willing to accept whatever the divine voice may have to say. Find the wind currents of the divine and glide that way.

Penalty and Plague

The biblical concept of holiness is not well understood apart from a particular understanding of the word "sin." It is important to be aware that the Bible views sin as a *relational* reality involving the God who loves and the human who chooses to embrace or violate that love relationship. If we were to think of sin as falling short of the complete will of a perfect God, all of us would necessarily remain unholy as long as we live. Rather, sin is a refusal to be bound to God's will, thus rupturing the divine-human relationship. It is the choice to eat the forbidden fruit, to breathe poisoned air.

Sin refers to a person turning away from God while holiness is the whole person turned in love toward God, making the self fully available to the cleansing and empowering work of the Holy Spirit. Conversion to Christ is a wonderful, forgiving work of the Spirit in the lives of humbled and repenting sinners. It is when guilt is acknowledged and a turn is made in the direction of the forgiving God. But there can, and must, be more.

John Wesley spoke of the possibility of an "entire" sanctification or a Christian "perfection" in this life. All is by God's grace and children of God are to be optimistic about the possibilities made possible by that grace—without ever bragging about spiritual achievements or claiming anything for themselves other than what God graciously gives. The "entire" of sanctification refers to the wholeness of the renewed relationship between a humbled heart and a healing God.

This first restorative move, conversion, is a critical turning. It addresses the *guilt* and *penalty* of sin. But conversion, the necessary beginning that turns and points one in the right direction, must proceed in the new, Godward direction. The new child of God must go on to experience the fullness of what that initial blessing promises. There is another exercise, really an extension of the first turn. One must turn toward God, first seeking forgiveness, and then also giving oneself wholly to God, seeking a deepening set-apartness and wholeness, a "sanctification" that cleanses and commissions.

This deepening involves a divine addressing of the *power* and *plague* of sin that can soon threaten, stunt, and rob converted believers of their joy and credibility as witnesses. We sinners do more than commit sin, requiring forgiveness; we also are infected by the sin disease, requiring a thorough change of our very characters. Turning toward God is the critical beginning; moving ahead in character transformation is the follow-up task and privilege of every serious believer. First, the car is washed, and then the tank is filled with fuel, all in preparation for a long and joyous journey.

How do we come to walk in this way of holiness? It is not merely the exercise of spiritual conversion, and then we are finally and fully there.

We must turn once and then continually move farther and farther away from the old to the new self. This moving on to spiritual wholeness usually has stages and requires time. Once turned from the sins of the past, there remains a lifelong spiritual journey of gaining a new being for the future. Forgiveness must move on to *character rebuilding*. Christ-like character is necessary and does not just happen. It is primarily the result of God's grace, of course, but grace that becomes coupled to our willing cooperation. We must *exercise* holiness by breathing in the Spirit.

Why the need for a lifelong journey? Why are new believers in Christ not automatically on the fast-track to holiness? It is because the world of sin includes both *penalty* and *plague*. We act wrongly and become guilty. We repent and are forgiven, released from the penalty of our particular sinful acts. This is the conversion turn. Then comes the larger awareness. Something is fundamentally wrong in our deepest being, something that caused the wrong acts in the first place. It has been called "original sin." It is the disease that plagues humans and needs cleansing and healing. To become holy is to address well the "I" issue.

As Galatians 2:20 says, the in-depth Christian life involves a moving of the "me" from the throne of life so that Christ is the One who comes to live within. The "saint" is the believer who has no selfish "I" left to project and always protect at the expense of others. The "I" has yielded to the "I Am" of God, allowing the emergence of a new self in Christ. For people who are transformed in this radical way, "perfect love" comes to casts out fear (1 John 4:18) since they no longer need to always be right in knowledge or performance. The comprehensive challenge is to be in *right relationship*. There is no more need for fear or disguise, no more playing public relations games to look righteous in the eyes of others. We can be freed by God's grace to be who we were meant to be—and now are actually becoming.

Of course, there is a starting point to this sanctification of the self—a moment when we decide that all of who we are will now be devoted to being all that God intends. But the start opens the door to a dynamic, ongoing relationship that continues to form our lives increasingly into the likeness of Christ. This is not merely doing the work of being prayerful in our private closets. This is truly the work of God in us. Even so, God chooses not to work alone. God provides, and we exercise our related responsibilities. We catch our spiritual breath and then we keep exhaling and inhaling in tune with the rhythm of the Spirit's ever-renewing life.

Pause that Refreshes

There is a necessary partnership that involves our choice to fully surrender ourselves to the Master. What the law did, according to Paul, was put a "band-aid on sin instead of a deep healing of it." Now that Christ has come, the right faith exercise is not "redoubling our own efforts" but gratefully embracing "what the Spirit is doing in us" (Rom. 8:4, The Message). According to Jesus, the first act of our partnership, after our repentance and being forgiven of the past, is to *wait on God* (Luke 24:49).

Athletes hate to pause. Isn't inactivity a poor way to play? They are trained to run, block, shoot, tackle, score! But, as my college basketball coach tried to teach me, the great players are the ones who know what to do *without having the ball*. It is a matter of anticipation and positioning. And it is no different in a Christian's spiritual life. Before the action and the attempt to score, there comes the critical question. What is the best instinctive, anticipated, and spiritual position on the floor? Alister McGrath unfortunately is right. "Evangelical" Christians are in real danger of being so busy doing things for God that they crowd God out of their very activities: "Our desire to do things for God can easily get in the way of God's desire to do something for us."[44] We must move to the holy position already provided in the game's design.

Jesus had returned to his Father. His physical absence threatened the very existence of the early church. What would be left when he was gone?

Then came the core message of Pentecost: *Jesus is not gone*! Yes, he was killed, resurrected, and ascended out of this world, but he is still here. The birthday of Jesus had led to a crucifixion day, then to resurrection and departure days, and finally, fifty days after Easter, to another birthday. Pentecost is the birthday of the church of Jesus, with the Spirit of God throwing the big party that celebrates the fresh and continuing presence of Jesus.

The enduring link between the Jesus of ancient Jewish history and Jesus of this hour is the *powerful presence of the Spirit of God*. Those first believers had done what Jesus told them to do. In his absence, they were not to take matters into their own hands. Instead, they got in the right, the holy position. They retreated, prayed, and waited until they were "clothed with power from on high" by the Spirit's powerful coming (Luke 24:49). This waiting business is difficult for us activist Christians. We want to plan, not pray, wade right into things, not wait on God. Nonetheless, according to Psalm 127:1, "Unless the Lord builds the house, those who build it labor in vain."

Several years ago engineers were building a new bridge over the East River in New York City. They discovered that the hull of a sunken ship lay right where the center piers of the bridge were to be built. Big cranes were brought in to remove the ship, but it would not budge from the mud of the river's floor. Then one of the engineers had an unusual idea—why not have the tide raise the ship? At low tide, huge cables were attached to the massive obstruction and to a big barge floating just above it. Then, as the tide came in, the barge gradually rose, and the wreck below lifted with it, unable to resist the power of the sea.

The lesson here? The mission of Christ in the world can be accomplished only by the power of the Spirit of Christ, the power of the divine sea. Our church-related ideas and programs and machines and institutions often fail. What will succeed? Life *in* the Spirit should precede ministry *through* the Spirit. We are to be Pentecost people in this world. That requires first having been in an upper room where the fire fell and hearts were set ablaze. The void in dead spiritual lungs must be filled with divine breath before world proclamation can begin.

In the fire of the Spirit, mere religion dissolves, authentic spirituality emerges, and the holy life of God begins to shine forth. Crucial for Christians is the exercise of climbing up the stairs to that upper room and kneeling there until it happens, until we catch our breath. Here is what we should be praying as we wait in that sacred place:

> Blessed are we when we do not have our hands on the steering wheels of our own lives. "Let me be *a feather on the breath of God.*"[45] Lord, help me to lighten myself, drop the weights of pride and prejudice and program fatigue, and prepare to flutter into this world on the breath and breeze of your Pentecostal Spirit! Come, Holy Spirit, come and dance as fire on my head. Pour the love of Jesus into me. Clarify Christ's teachings in my mind. Burn Christ's mission into my heart. O, Spirit of the eternities, blow over this place as I kneel. Set me on fire with your love. Make the language of your love understood by everyone through me. Make the church of Jesus the community of the Spirit, the church truly *of God*.

Being forgiven by God, *initial* sanctification, deals with sin's *guilt* and *penalty*. It is our essential beginning, a qualitative change, a new birth as spiritual beings in Christ. Then comes spiritual growth and maturing, first in the decision in an upper room to allow the Spirit to reign in love, *entire* sanctification, and then, *progressive* sanctification, an ongoing dealing with sin's *plague* and *power*. The changes are in degree—with the relationship potentially whole all the way.

The heart, already born of God, can come to be purified in love, gaining an ever-greater likeness to Christ and finding an ever-greater potential in Christ's service. Even those purified are still in the growth process—after all, sanctified believers, those who have waited and allowed the inward work of the Spirit, always remain fallible humans journeying upward with Christ. *Total* sanctification awaits the glorified state beyond this fleshly life.

This ongoing growth in grace is to become love's passion and must be intentionally nurtured. All is of God, of course, always, although much is to happen in our *responsive partnership* with God. God is a living and *relating* God who expects responsibility on the part of his grace-blessed children.

Partners in Progress

Spiritual progress is not accidental or automatic. Holiness must be breathed, exercised. It is a relationship with God that must be nurtured. The relationship involves a partnership between God's enabling graciousness and our responding faithfulness. God speaks, directs, and provides; we hear, follow, exercise, and serve. In John Wesley's sermon "On Working Out Our Own Salvation," he makes clear that salvation is a partnership, but also that God *first* works in us and then calls on us to join in that work of amazing grace.

The New Testament refers often to this partnership—both God's initiation and then the importance of our exercising appropriate responsiveness.

We are told to "run with perseverance the race that is set before us" (Heb. 12:1). Jesus said to a man with a withered hand, "Stretch out your hand" (Luke 6:10). The man exercised his unused muscles and the hand was restored—it would not have been healed if the man would have refused to do the stretching.

Paul urged the church in Philippi to "work out your own salvation with fear and trembling, for it is God who is at work in you, enabling you both to will and to work for his good pleasure" (Phil. 2:12). God grants the salvation; we exercise a partnership that helps activate its coming and development. God blows and we manage to catch our breath.

There is no one clear formula by which the Spirit forms us into fully mature spiritual people. Holiness people have been criticized for having a set spiritual formula, a definite "method" by which people should/will experience grace and growth. For instance, some insist these are "two works of grace" (salvation and sanctification), and they must be received in given ways and times—even places (on one's knees at an altar in front of a large crowd). Even though there are two needs (sin's penalty and plague), the steps that most of us take toward holiness are hardly mechanical and uniform. There are many variables. We should focus on the goal, not the particulars of location, emotion, timing, etc., often mere human expectations.

The picture of the salvation-holiness process as taught by John Wesley, fountainhead of the Methodist tradition, is more one of "Way" than of "Order" (although it is both). The latter suggests a series of discrete states and steps that are linked together like a fixed chain. The former speaks more of a growing, mutual, and responsive relationship between the "saved" and the "Savior." Wesley's long teaching career reflects some of the "Order" approach, particularly in its earlier stages; but in its later stage there was more emphasis on the gradual nature of salvation and the dynamics of its development. The Christian life was seen "as a continuing journey into increasing depths of 'grace upon grace'."[46]

BUT NOT SO FAST!

The grace of God, while given freely, does not eliminate our human responsibility. Not at all. We are responsible because divine grace increases our response-*ability*. As our ability increases because of grace, we become increasingly responsible to be active partners with God in our continuing salvation process. And what is the goal of this divine-human partnership? It is what lay at the center of Wesley's concept of "sanctification," the "graciously-empowered formation of Christ-like character."[47] Christian life is not merely being marked by forgiveness of the sin-guilt problem. It also is Christ being formed in us so that we become "little Christs" to others.

Christian disciples are both *born* and *made*. The "means of grace" are those spiritual disciplines or exercises offered by God as ways we can partner in our ongoing spiritual formation (see chapter 9). The effect of a free-flowing of the Master's life in us is that we become *like him*. We become filled with the Master's character; we become "Master-full." How can "sanctified" believers be spotted? They are the ones whose confidence is no longer in themselves, but in Christ, whose security is no longer in their own ability to achieve, but in Christ, whose energy is no longer sapped by trying to measure up, but who are relaxed in the gracious embrace of divine love.[48]

Organized religion is a fundamental fact of human life, ancient and modern. What is most important to us humans, life's meaning and our happiness and final destiny, get packaged into "sacred" creeds, practices, and institutions. This packaging seems inevitable and certainly can be very important. We need a community of faith, help along the way, "means" and structures for divine grace to flow to and through us. But established religion also can be dangerous and distracting to faith's successful journey. The road of "religion" can be rough indeed!

Religion is supposed to teach, guide, and coordinate our search for meaning, happiness, and destiny, our gaining of "salvation." Too often, however, organized religion turns our quest into patterns of approved achievement through insistence that we belong to the right group, practice the right rituals, or believe exactly the right things as our denomination defines them. In fact, such church establishments are to be only "tugboats to get you away from the shore and out into the right sea; they are the oars to get you working and engaged with the Mystery. But never confuse these instruments with your profound 'ability to share in the divine nature' itself (2 Peter 1:4)."[49] The Mystery is God and the goal of "religion" is assisting us to gain a right relationship with God so that we actually share in that nature and engage in the work of that divine will.

Churches are divine-human institutions. I once wrote that "Christianity, beyond being a unique way of thinking, is a unique way of linking. The church is blessed with a measure of divinity, and also lives with much humanness.... Because the church is human it is subject to the limitations of people and time; because it is divine God enables it to rise above such persistent limitations.... [The church] is a community of hope, a present reality created by the impact of the future made known in the history of Jesus. It lives between the times and between the worlds."[50]

The church in its organized forms is important to our full exercising of holiness, but the church is never God. Paul soon announced to the early church, "I have been crucified with Christ; and it is no longer I who live, but it is Christ who lives in me" (Gal. 2:20). Believers are to "have this mind in you that was also in Christ Jesus" (Phil. 2:5). He was calling for believers to pray for Pentecostal presence and power, seeking to receive and not manufacture it. Church life in this world is important, but never to be *our show*. It is God's family, an intended aid to our spiritual lives and a vehicle for our coordinated service for Christ.

Pentecost involves waiting for and yielding to the coming Spirit of God. It is the pause that refreshes. You may have heard of training sessions for tongues speaking—don't go. You may have heard of miracle handbooks for guaranteed church growth. Read them if you want, but with great care. The birthing and gifting of the church are *God's doing*, not ours. Real progress relies on the Spirit's coming, not our coming and doing. Pentecost is never found on the web site with the address "I_Did_It_My_Way.com."

The ".com" likely suggests that someone is selling something, and the presence of God's Spirit is never for sale. We are to do things the Spirit's way.

So, how do we get the mind of Jesus in us, the presence and power and breath of the Spirit in us, the church to really be *God's church*? Jesus gave the answer to his disciples. He said, "I will not leave you orphaned.... I will ask the Father, and he will give you another Advocate—my own Spirit breath, to be with you forever. This is the Spirit of truth" (John 14:16-18). The central holiness exercise is to open our hearts and lungs and receive and breathe this Spirit.

CHAPTER 7

RHYTHMS OF THE SPIRIT

Sing songs to the tune of his glory, set glory to the rhythms of his praise (Psalm 66:2, The Message). Jesus said: "Walk with me and work with me—watch how I do it. Learn the unforced rhythms of grace" (Matt. 11:29, The Message).

John Wesley's most explicit delineation of the three dimensions of human salvation are *pardon*, salvation begun, *holiness*, salvation continued, and *heaven*, salvation finished.[51] Salvation is a process of staying in rhythm with the transforming work of the Spirit, breathing in tune with the melody of heaven.

We already have covered considerable basic ground. Salvation is not simple, not a one-time event, and not only a dealing with the guilt for past sins. Salvation includes Christian holiness as its larger goal—not just being forgiven, but having had re-established in our innermost beings a pervasive Christ-likeness. As seen in the quotes above, the Christian life has growth stages, rhythms of grace, walking, working, watching, breathing, and learning requirements. The goal is the wholeness of renewed relationship.

Holiness is more than a legal acquittal of sin and a pattern of doing many right things. It also is a matter of new character formation, the emergence of a truly new self in Christ. Sin should be understood both as specific past acts and the prevailing human condition. The new self in Christ is realized when the humbled person repents of wrongdoing and then also turns the whole self toward God, making it available for cleansing, indwelling, empowerment, and commissioning by the Holy Spirit. First, wait and wonder, and then work.

To be holy, one must dare to stop and hold still, let go and let God, exhale death and inhale life. This enables the believer to get into the right rhythm, to be released into the divine flow of things. Holiness is that higher ground where a steady faith perspective is fixed on eternity and has a view of things that can ride out storms and see the sun shining beyond dark clouds.

There are valuable "rhythms of praise" to God as well as "rhythms of grace" needing to be learned and followed. To be holy, one must dare to stop and hold still, let go and let God, exhale death and inhale life. This enables the believer to get into the right rhythm, to be released into the divine flow of things. The Christian life is a gift *and* a task, something both received and accomplished. Holiness is not a long list of moral absolutes and prohibitions, but a love relationship involving a significant partnership between God and the believer.

Spiritual formation requires an intentional exhaling of the old self and an inhaling of the new self that wills only what God wills. It is a life deliberately on journey toward more and more spiritual maturity and fruitfulness. It is a life beating with God's heart, flowing with God's breath, and increasingly being an instrument in tune with the rhythm of God's Spirit.

We now explore aspects of this ongoing spiritual journey. There is to be an increasing rhythm to life that blends the life movements of growing believers with the movements of God's Spirit. There are particular movements of the Spirit, and holiness is the result of sensing these movements and choosing to flow with the stream of life-giving grace. Christian growth involves breathing with the Spirit who blows graciously over our lives. The rhythm centers in exhaling the stuff of death, inhaling the Spirit of life, and singing praises of thanksgiving in tune with God's great salvation song.

Man for All Seasons

The play *A Man for All Seasons* by Robert Bolt is about Sir Thomas More. He was a man in Henry VIII's English court who stepped out of line. He thought it was wrong for the king to manipulate the pope in order to secure an annulment of his marriage, allowing him to marry Anne Boleyn. More's opposition shows the subtle clash of the known of human ways and the relatively unknown ways of God. He relied on the devices and securities of this world while also being quietly swept out to sea by allegiance to the less-known world of the spirit. Trying to be a man for all seasons finally led More to his execution.

Jesus also was a man for all seasons in ways well beyond the principled Sir Thomas More. He knew the Father, challenged the world's ways, and finally also faced execution. But Jesus was more than a political philosopher with a conscience; he was God with us, the One showing us how to negotiate life in this world. He was a man for all needs and times.

Archimedes, inventor of the lever and pulley, classically said, "Give me a place to stand and I will move the earth." The more modern D. Elton Trueblood extended this observation to Christian faith, arguing that the ultimate act of a reasoned faith is to exercise affirmation of the full trustworthiness of Jesus Christ. Here is the place where we can stand and from which we can change the world, although not without risk. Jesus is the firm and perennial fulcrum of our faith.[52]

The unrivaled man from Nazareth knew sorrow and yet overflowed with joy. He stood boldly for the right at the cost of his own life, and yet was hospitable to an amazing array of sinners. He loved lonely places and yet appeared at times in the middle of crowds, even being the life of the party. He was a man of the mountains and the valleys, confrontational when necessary and yet silent as a sacrificial lamb in the face of a demanding Pilate. Jesus remains "with us when we soar on wings as eagles… and…when we can't walk for fainting. And everywhere in between…. Our hearts taste the rapture and leisure of summer, the industry and urgency of fall, the bleakness and loneliness of winter, the busyness and expectancy of spring."[53] His disciples must learn the resilience and balance of his ways, the "unforced rhythms of grace" (Matt. 11:29, The Message).

My wife and I have been in various African countries surrounded by severe poverty and numerous orphans created by the scourge of AIDS. We also have been blessed by choirs of orphaned children singing in celebration of the care they now are receiving. They sing and dance with a distinctive African beat and rhythm that temporarily sets aside the sordidness of the setting and lets great joy come through. Likewise, eternity lurks just beneath the pain or glory, beauty or ugliness of each season of life. To be holy is to be rooted in that eternity enough to be able to move through life's changes and crises with a God-inspired balance and stability.

Holiness is that higher ground where a steady faith perspective is fixed on eternity and has a view of things that can ride out storms and see the sun shining beyond dark clouds. The Jews knew first the grief and drudgery of exile and then the exhilaration of the prophet's announcement that they were about to go home to Jerusalem (Isaiah 40). The disciples of Jesus had experienced the shock of their Lord dying on a cross only to hear the announcement that he had risen! They learned that staying close to him is wisdom, strength, and the future.

Our spiritual goal as Christians is to learn to flow with the distinctive rhythm of each season of life and faith. Something that sustained the exiled Jews and then the commissioned disciples was a hymnody that we have come to call the Book of Psalms. It is a collection of sung prayers that fit virtually any stage or occasion of faith—or doubt. There are seasons of the heart and the challenge is to be aware of Christ's presence in season and out, singing even in the darkness that finally cannot hide the light.

The writer of Ecclesiastes says that for everything there is a season even though so much can appear futile and empty at first glance. But the end of the matter is fearing God, keeping his commandments, and knowing that one day "God will bring every deed into judgment, including every secret thing, whether good or evil" (Ecc. 12:14). John begins his story of Jesus by announcing that "the light shines in the darkness and the darkness did not overcome it" (John 1:5). Faith knows that, whatever the present circumstances, God's light will always shine and the divine breath will always be available.

> *Spiritually mature believers certainly can grow in wisdom as they breathe in the Spirit and exercise holiness more and more, but there are limits. The paradox is real. We use our minds to the full and yet know their significant limitations. We "saints" become aware of the rhythm of knowing and not knowing. We come to know more and more, and also less and less. We grow ever more sensitive to life's great questions, and yet more hesitant to offer quick and simplistic answers to these questions.*

Choosing the Right Fear

Faith involves "fearing" God, kneeling in awe of the Holy One. To inhale the divine breath enables liberation and new birth, but only with our willing choice to live with the right fear.

For today's self-assured and scientifically-oriented people, one essential spiritual lesson is not learned easily. We tend to deny what is not readily available to our senses and controllable by our rational minds and human powers. Even so, Christian spiritual formation must begin by our choosing the right fear. What is it? We are weak, wounded, limited people. Our human powers are so inadequate for the biggest issues of life. We know this and try to relieve our anxiety by covering up the inadequacy with masks of confidence.

The stark fact is that we fear failing in life and being found out by those around us. When it comes to God, we want to know fully and even control as much as possible. But, in fact, such things cannot be. We must learn to "fear" God and begin to find that in this holy and humble reverence there lays adequacy, hope, joy, peace, and rest.

Spiritual growth happens when we come to terms with God's *incomprehensibility*. We "advanced" people of the twenty-first century face a hard fact. We cannot become "experts" in the things of God. God is greater than our minds and cannot be captured in our words, thoughts, practices, and religious institutions. Real spiritual learning begins when we reach the point of understanding and accepting a great paradox. Saints of the past have called it *docta ignorantia*, an articulate *not-knowing*, an unusual wisdom rooted in a deep humility.

The spiritually mature certainly can grow in wisdom as they breathe in the Spirit and exercise holiness more and more, but there are limits. The paradox is real. We use our minds to the full and yet know their significant limitations. We "saints" become aware of the rhythm of knowing and not knowing. We come to know more and more, and also less and less. We grow ever more sensitive to life's great questions, and yet more hesitant to offer quick and simplistic answers to these questions.

Our relationships become more intense and meaningful, and what knowledge we do have sweetens into increased satisfaction. We stop fearing ignorance and rest in what we do know, and that is primarily our trust in God as known in Jesus Christ. The rest for our souls comes because Jesus proves to be adequate in every season, including the seasons of our ignorance and doubts and disappointments.

With spiritual maturity comes an increased appreciation of silence. Solitude is drained of its fear. Like Jesus, we long for the gentle rest of isolation, not to escape, but always in preparation for returning to the crowds better prepared for ministry purposes. Our new and loving nature causes us to reach out and link with others more readily. The following wisdom begins to make great sense to us: "Once a person moves to deep time, he or she is utterly one with the whole communion of saints and sinners, past and future (a good way to understand reincarnation!). In deep time, everybody matters...and is even somehow 'present' and not just past."[54]

Being increasingly mature spiritually—being holy—brings with it important insights regarding our understanding of God. God becomes an ever greater source of transcendent amazement, and also an ever more intimate friend. God grows in our experience as more known, while remaining the Eternal Mystery. We come to "know" with increasing confidence, while we are increasingly aware that all is *by faith*. Faith becomes less the supposition that *something* might be true, exactly as we have thought it out, and more the assurance that *Someone* really is there—and there *for us*. To the mature child of God, the Heavenly Father is closer than can be described, and yet more distant than can be comprehended by the most brilliant theologian. God becomes less the "object" of our knowledge and more the comforting source of our wonder!

Isaiah 6 offers a window through which we can catch a vision of the biblical understanding of holiness. It involves confrontation with the divine. There come from this confrontation important realizations, a new reverence, and a stretching toward new life that includes a divine commission.

The Holy God is calling for a holy people who are on a divine mission and are being propelled by a divine breath that they will never fully understand and certainly will never control.

Like Isaiah of old, we are to humble ourselves and be overwhelmed by a vision of the holy God. We are to open ourselves to the divine presence, be humbled, touched, purified, and gripped by the desire to live out of this transforming experience—"here am I; send me!" (Isaiah 6:8). We must exercise the right fear, that of a deeply reverent and profoundly grateful servant. Such a believer will never have the desired answers to many of life's questions (at least not in this life), and yet will lack nothing of significance and will have enough assurance to keep going.

It might help to listen in on a conversation that might have happened in the womb of a woman soon to deliver twins. The twins temporarily residing in this dark place are discussing the best available future for themselves. The sister risks a daring idea, her belief that there is *life after birth*. The brother is skeptical. After all, neither of them has seen anything but the dark, cozy place where they are. His view was simple and practical. Hang on to that cord that feeds and be content there forever. Skip any wild speculation. The only thing known so far is likely the only thing there is to be known.

For some reason, and despite the brother's cynicism, the sister had become convinced that there must be a bigger place with lots of light. She even suggested that there might be a mother, not just the two of them, and a source of nourishment other that their treasured cord. Even though the brother scoffed at such folly, she persisted. Had they not both felt some strange squeezing that she judged an uncomfortable way of getting them ready to exit into a bright new world, one where a mother would be waiting to welcome them. After all, the squeezing was getting stronger and surely it had some purpose. Could she be right? A brighter world? A real mother? Surely not. But maybe. And then it happened![55]

Holiness is a little like that. It is the opposite of grasping the little security we have known so far, all ego-centered. It is an attitude of faith that senses a new future coming and is committed to it. It feels the squeezing and is sure that it is the way to new life. It knows the pain of helplessness and yet believes that there is One who is about to deliver and will provide. It hears a heartbeat not its own and is sure that, as the minutes come and go, something really special is on the way. Love is in the wind and life waits in another place. At the moment of birth, the lungs often are clogged. But the great Someone will be there to help the baby catch its breath and begin to live well in a very different place.

Holiness is rooted in an optimistic expectation and a holy fear, but not a fear that fosters guilt in the face of God's awful judgment. "Be afraid," shouts the condemning preacher, "because God will punish you horribly if you do not do the right thing, and do it right now exactly as I say!" Instead, the psalmist calls us to come and exercise the holy fear of the Lord (Psalm 34:11). "O fear the Lord, you his holy ones" (Psalm 34:9). God seeks to lead us to a fear, a holy fear, that wonderfully relieves all other fears.

Fear God? Yes, but we are not being called to hide from the great avenger, to shake when God gets too near and judgment looms. We are being called to a path of wisdom, to a life-giving fear of proper reverence. We tell our children not to drink from any bottle stored under the sink. Our purpose is not to give them nightmares, not to stunt their lives, keeping them from more and more options that would quench their thirst. Not at all. We are seeking to protect and enrich their lives by teaching them wisdom—the difference between good and bad drinks.

God told his first children not to eat of one particular tree, not because he wanted to restrict their diets, but because he wanted to preserve their very lives (Gen. 2 and 3). Living with a holy fear means being able to fall and fail without falling apart. The threat of death tends to trouble the people who have not yet really lived. If we have deepened like Jesus "in wisdom and in years and in divine and human favor" (Luke 2:52), any crippling fear tends to recede. We have known life and no longer fear death. We have feared God and found all other fears to be fading away.

"Salvation" should not be understood as a reluctant acceptance of God's many, life-choking *don'ts*; it is to be the breath releasing and joyfully accepting of the opportunity to be part of a great reversal that leads to new life opportunities. Humans have ignored "mommy" and swallowed drain-cleaner from under life's sink. God now says, "Come to me, trust my judgment, receive my cure, drink the purest water, and live!" Salvation reverses the sin disaster with a life-giving drink of grace.

Drink of God, "fear" God, and return to real life refreshed. Jesus said to the woman at Jacob's well, "Everyone who drinks of this water will be thirsty again, but those who drink of the water that I will give them will never be thirsty. The water that I will give will become in them a spring of water gushing up to eternal life" (John 4:13-14).

There is a positive, a holy, a healing fear. The very being of God has been called a tremendous and fascinating mystery. Rudolf Otto called it our sensing of a *mysterium tremendum*. The mystery comes from God always being beyond our full comprehension—if we could comprehend, and thus control, we would ourselves be God! But, as known most fully in Jesus, God is truly fascinating, always beyond, comfortingly near, irresistibly magnetic, a love that attracts and draws us in without itself being reduced to our creaturely level.

The fear of God should drip with respect and gratitude. Salvation should present itself to us as a life-giving stream filled with willing obedience, enhanced dignity, fresh air, and comforting hope. To be holy is to be bathed in this stream and flowing with its pulsating current. To be alive is to be breathing in rhythm with the Spirit of God.

Those rendered holy by their fresh existence in this joyful fascination with the loving and redeeming God are, in one sense, fearless. Why? They have risen above fear because of their having embraced the right fear. Says the psalmist, "Those who fear him have no want" (Psalm 34:1). The humbled, the holy ones, willingly, happily, joyfully seek peace, do good, and depart from evil. They want no more of that under-the-sink existence that leads only to death. They need not fear any contaminants in the fresh water that Jesus gives. They have exhaled death and are inhaling life!

Breathing Cycles

My wife and I recently attended the concert of a famous group of five men called the *Canadian Brass*. They were superb musicians who also entertained with their physical humor. At one point, they decided to play and act out a ballet—it was outrageously uncoordinated and brought bursts of laughter and a standing ovation. Good music and certainly ballet—the real kind—requires precise attention to rhythm. Everything seems to. There is even the "rhythm method" of family planning. One must take a calendar and follow with care the cycles of key bodily functions if unwanted conceptions are to be avoided—an inexact science that is better than nothing.

One especially insightful writer, in exploring the Christian's spiritual life, has identified critical cycles of exhaling the old and inhaling the new. Henri Nouwen points to the breathing cycles of opaqueness to transparency, illusion to prayer, sorrow to joy, resentment to gratitude, fear to love, exclusion to inclusion, and denying to befriending death.[56] Each of these holy paths moves one forward in a particular aspect of life. Each brings a maturing believer deeper into the Christ-life, and thus brings more growth and freedom, more holiness.

One helpful way of picturing a Christian's deep knowing and healthy spiritual breathing is becoming aware of the right place in which to live our spiritual lives. There is a particular house of religion into which we must enter and live. This house is the subject of the next chapter.

LETTING GOD:
INHALING

CHAPTER 8

LIVING IN THE RIGHT HOUSE

Come to him, a living stone, though rejected by mortals yet chosen and precious in God's sight, and like living stones, let yourselves be built into a spiritual house, to be a holy priesthood, to offer spiritual sacrifices acceptable to God through Jesus Christ (1 Peter 2:4-5).

O Lord, who may abide in your tent? Who may dwell on your holy hill? Those who walk blamelessly, and do what is right, and speak the truth from their heart (Psalm 15:1-2).

True dwellers are true breathers, and it is only God who gives breath to his people (Isaiah 42:5).

Christian holiness can be pictured helpfully as believers in Jesus finding the right house of faith to live in and taking seriously the process of actually moving in. According to the biblical references above, Christ is the foundation, the residents are its building materials, and all who live there must walk blamelessly if they are to remain.

The Best Address

Where do you exercise? It may be a favorite track around which you jog, or a stationery exercise machine placed in front of a television set. Many people go to a gymnasium or health club, houses built especially for entertainment, competition, or physical well being. Where do you choose to live? We must be careful to go through the right doors and into the right house. There are plenty of houses designed for our destruction (dare I mention casinos, taverns, brothels, etc.?). One is a divine dwelling open to all.

There are various biblical references to "houses" in which God lives, beginning with the Tabernacle described in Exodus 25. First Peter speaks of the potential of believers in Jesus being, themselves, built into spiritual houses in which holiness can dwell. God can and will dwell in us and walk with us (2 Cor. 6:16). What an amazing possibility, a habitat for humanity built with the best of everything and owned by the Lord of all land!

> God's saints will exercise openness to the voice and wisdom of the Spirit; they will make room for their fellow believers, different or not; and they will be anxious for friendship with those still outside the faith, hostile or not. To live in God's house is to breathe the Spirit's air and be involved in the Spirit's life and mission.

The whole life of faith can be thought of as a house. John Wesley spoke of a house of religion with various parts representing stages of faith and personal transformation. To be built into a truly spiritual house is to take advantage of all parts of the faith structure and experience in relation to all aspects of our lives. Unfortunately, so many of us do little in our walks of faith other than look at God's house, or maybe go up and sit on the porch and rock. Holiness requires accepting the divine invitation and actually moving in.

Wesley sorrowed at mere house-watching and house-sitting. He made his dismay plain in the sermon "The Mystery of Iniquity." Many professing to be Christian in his day looked and acted much like those with no profession of faith. His emphasis on the potential of the holy life through the power of divine grace was an attempt to change this serious situation. Wesley believed that, for those willing to exercise an unqualified commitment to Jesus Christ, God would provide the means to live a truly holy life—getting from the rocking chair on the porch to places well inside the house. Like living stones, those who *will* surely *can* be built into a spiritual house (1 Peter 2:4-5). Those who occupy the house of faith and are built into the house will receive the fruit of "scriptural Christianity."

Walking Inside the Christ House

What summarizes the essence of the Christian spiritual life as it ought to be? Henri Nouwen has answered well: "To live in the world without belonging to the world.... The spiritual life keeps us aware that our true house is not the house of fear, in which the powers of hatred and violence rule, but the house of love, where God resides."[57] God is love. All who choose to dwell inside God's house will necessarily dwell in love.

Dwelling in love is living the holy life. Such life involves certain exercises, three of which are explored in the remainder of this chapter. In brief, God's saints will exercise *openness* to the voice and wisdom of the Spirit; they will *make room* for their fellow believers, different or not; and they will *be anxious* for friendship with those still outside the faith, hostile or not. To live in God's house is to breathe the Spirit's air and be involved in the Spirit's life and mission.

The religious house can be a holy dwelling containing all the essentials of Christian doctrine and life if it is filled with God's presence and love. The essentials are repentance, faith, and holiness. The most important roles of the Bible and God's Spirit are to guide and enable us on the paths of spiritual formation—to the house, on to the porch in repentance, through the door of faith, and into the sanctifying atmosphere of the many rooms inside. To be all that God desires involves the home exercises of going up the front steps, swinging open the front door, and walking expectantly deep inside the dwelling.

Our personal journeys involve house-entering stages. The initial contact with holiness is first becoming convicted of our sin through the work of the Holy Spirit. This "porch" should lead to our repentance of sin, our forgiveness by God, and then to our fresh desire to walk boldly through the door of faith into the spiritual riches of the home's interior. Love is the heart of holiness, the hallways within, the goal of faith, the highest level of life in Christ. The door of the house opens into a purifying love. It is a crossing of the porch and a passing by faith through the door which Wesley called the "handmaid of love."

Robert Barclay was the early intellectual of English Quakerism. He maintained that there is no real church without a serious expectation of a

> *Going into the house of faith is a must. It is like coming up from the water of baptism and catching a fresh breath of new life. There is death before life (going down, exhaling) and then new life after the old self is abandoned (coming up, inhaling the Spirit's breath). With the Spirit allowed to blow freely, so much comes flowing into the living spaces of our faith. We exhale the stale air that has exhausted oxygen. We inhale the breath of Christ, taking it in deeply and regularly.*

moral difference, a character change in the lives of its members. It is not enough to settle for a "forensic" assurance of forgiveness of sins—a courtroom decision that we are now absolved of guilt and free to go our way as we choose. Such assurance can be surface only, numbed and paralyzed if we fail to recognize the purpose of our forgiveness. We are set free of guilt in order to be set on the road to holiness—which leads right into the house.

This holiness road can be dangerous in our kind of world. John Wesley was very concerned that his early Methodists would join England's growing middle class, get economically comfortable, and settle for the mere externals and traditions of the faith. He knew that they could not be spiritually happy and whole (holy) by feeding only on shallow and formal religious things any more than a man can "fill his belly with the east wind." Holiness is the real food.

Going into the house of faith is a must. It is like coming up from the water of baptism and catching a fresh breath of new life. There is death before life (going down, exhaling) and then new life after the old self is abandoned (coming up, inhaling the Spirit's breath). Paul refers to the death and resurrection of Jesus as a pointed analogy. With God's Spirit alive in you, "your body will be as alive as Christ's" (Rom. 8:11, The Message).

The righteousness for which we must thirst is "the life which is hid with Christ in God," the one having "fellowship with the Father and the Son," and the one "walking in the light as God is in the light," thus being "purified even as He is pure."[58] As we have seen in our own time, Wesley observed in his life that many people live the Christian life as if it were only the porch and door of religion's house. They never go inside! He challenged the early Methodists to "go on to perfection," to enter, enjoy, and rejoice. As we explained in chapter 5, we should not hesitate at the word perfection, awkward as it is. Passing through faith's door is an act of humility and obedience, a continuing reception of God's unmerited grace, the answering of a divine invitation.

Of course, once inside we will not manage to explore all the rooms of this house in our earthly lifetimes. No matter. We are called to pass through the door, yield to the joys and demands of love, and keep going from room to room, moving on to perfection as God's grace enables and our faithfulness permits. This going in and then going on involves a life of loving service shaped and directed by God's own Spirit. Holiness brings us to the porch of religion's house (conviction of sin), takes us through the door of faith that is made of forgiveness (conversion), and over time directs us into and around the many rooms of the house's amazing interior (spiritual formation).

The word "sanctification" refers to going deeper into the faith, deep enough to begin reaping the benefits of actually living "in Christ," a favorite holiness phrase of the Apostle Paul. This phrase appears in every letter of Paul except 2 Thessalonians. It carries what Paul understood to be the heart of Christian life—and not only for first-century disciples who knew Jesus in the flesh.[59] The phrase varies in form, sometimes being *in Christ*, *in Christ Jesus*, *in Jesus Christ*, or *in the Lord*, but never *in Jesus*. It does not point to a physical relationship dependent on location or time. Rather, it describes a relationship with the Spirit of Christ who is the everywhere existing and always present and truly risen Lord. Paul's greetings go to "every saint in Christ Jesus" (Phil. 4:21). To be whole, holy, a true saint, is to be *in Christ Jesus*, in God's house.

Staying with the house metaphor, consider this sad scene. One of the more troubling objections to Christianity comes from non-believers who point to the failings of the Christians they know. The weakness of this objection is that these failing "believers" are lined up on the porch of religion, pleasantly rocking away and living much like those who claim no faith at all. A better judgment about Christianity would come by observing the relatively few who have left the porch, are hungering after righteousness, and are found only *inside*.

Sanctification is actually going inside and becoming part of the residence. Being inside is the only place where we begin to really catch our breath and experience personally the testimony of Paul: "It is no longer I who live, but it is Christ who lives in me. And the life I now live in the flesh I live by faith in the Son of God, who loved me and gave himself for me" (Gal. 2:20). This is a witness to the spiritual reality that resides only deep inside the house. It is having the mind of Christ, breathing the breath of Christ, and living the life of Christ before others (Phil. 2:1-11). It is saying "Yes!" to the gracious offerings of God. According to Paul, Jesus always said yes and *was yes* in relation to all of God's promises (2 Cor. 1:20). To this, Paul and we are to say "Amen" to the glory of God!

Holiness is not to be a life of no-saying, but the exhilaration of yes-saying to the promises and possibilities of God. Sanctification is being "set apart." Believers must be *set apart* before they are *sent out* to witness and serve. Effective ministry is the Spirit breathing and acting lovingly through us. Since we are to be instruments and channels of the Spirit, Spirit-infilling is crucial for Spirit-sharing. Jesus commissioned his disciples to go and make disciples of all the nations (Matt. 28:19). But he explained that, before they set out, they first should wait to be truly set apart. They should "stay here in the city until you have been clothed with power from on high" (Luke 24:49). Disciples are to be receivers before they are givers.

John Wesley explained that we come to the Lord's Table (communion) or the Lord's tabernacle (house) not to give anything to God "but to receive whatsoever he sees best for us, [so that] there is no previous preparation indispensably necessary but a desire to receive whatsoever he pleases to give." Holiness is not our doing all the right things as much as receiving all of God's good things. Holiness is not a collection of mandated outward characteristics, like wearing the right clothes, relating only to the right people, doing good for others, and being faithful to church services and functions and creeds. Rather, it is "the life of God in the soul; the image of God fresh stamped on the heart; an entire renewal of the mind in every temper and thought, after the likeness of Him that created it."[60] Holiness is choosing to go inside God's house and becoming a real resident, a truly new and Spirit-breathing person in Christ.

With the Windows Open

An elderly musician was reflecting on the many decades of change in the music world that he had seen during his long life. He admitted having altered his own musical style several times, trying to keep up with changing times. He then offered this quaint piece of wisdom. A person's mind, he said, works best when, like a parachute, it is opened! The wind must be caught.

What should a believer do once inside religion's house? Reflecting the wisdom of the elderly musician, we should actually open all of life to the wind of God—the life of faith works best that way. Healthy spiritual exercise must continue and needs fresh air constantly filling the lungs, with the sails of life positioned to catch that wind. This means keeping the windows of religion's house wide open. With the Spirit allowed to blow freely, so much comes flowing into the living spaces of our faith. We exhale the stale air that has exhausted oxygen. We inhale the breath of Christ, taking it in deeply and regularly.

We who believe and are faithful in our exhaling and inhaling come to experience many wonderful things—the "highs" that follow good exercise. We have consolation in Christ (Phil. 2:1). We become bold in Christ (Philem. 8), gain liberty in Christ (Gal. 2:4), acquire truth in Christ (Rom. 9:1), and learn to live from the promises in Christ (Eph. 3:6). Only in Christ do we grow wise (1 Cor. 4:10), become new creatures (2 Cor. 5:17), and find ourselves being "sanctified" (1 Cor. 1:2). These are all inside-the-house possibilities.

Christians living in Christ exercise holiness by throwing open the windows of their individual hearts and various fellowships. Hurtful disunity among Christians is so un-Christ-like and would largely disappear if we would only realize that being truly Christian does not necessarily mean being in a particular church body, confessing a particular theological creed, or doing sacred things in particular ways. Being truly Christian means keeping windows open, being in Christ, and exercising for growth in him *together*.

We spoke earlier of a "saint" as being a believer truly living "in Christ." An important result of such living is coming to realize that, in the sacred space defined by Christ, there no longer are the usual human distinctions (discriminations) of Jew *or* Greek, male *or* female, bond *or* free (Gal. 3:28). Why? Because all Christians, the in-Christ ones and the inside-the-house ones, are *one body in Christ* (Rom. 12:5). Our primary identification once on the inside cannot be "Catholic" or "Baptist" or "Methodist," but "Christian." Actually, true believers are sometimes hesitant to even carry the label Christian, not wanting to be associated with all of the historic failings of Christianity as a formalized religion. A good alternative would be "a follower of Jesus."[61]

I come from a Christian tradition sensitive to the historic evils of denominationalism. Structures—even church structures/denominations—can, and often do, become self-serving, myopic, lacking genuine catholicity. On the other hand, lack of reasonable structure in church life can, and often does, disintegrate into chaotic individualism that is very different from the community-based nature of the Judeo-Christian faith tradition. All Christians must inhabit the same house of true religion, with only the name of Jesus Christ over the door. They also must live inside some particular Christian tradition, of course. The goal is not to eradicate all traditional differences of belief, practice, and historic memory, but to keep open the windows of one's tradition so that cooperative learning, sharing, and serving is a natural and frequent occurrence.

We all need fresh air to breath. For a particular faith community (congregation or denomination) to isolate itself from the larger body of Christ is to commit the arrogant sin of terrible body management. None of us has all the truth and does everything just right. Any isolation inside "our" church house can starve the larger church's lungs of the wind of the Spirit, which blows wherever it chooses—including outside our artificial church boundaries.

Pastors so easily get overwhelmed with their demanding work and become isolated and frustrated. Many denominations have programs for nurturing leaders who are in mid-career or transition or on the edge of a burn-out. In my church, the program is called *SHAPE* (Sustaining Health and Pastoral Excellence). Wellness, unity, and growth come when church leaders become vulnerable to caring colleagues so that they can journey together toward more open, honest, and fulfilling lives and ministries. All disciples must keep the windows open to each other!

The most famous and beloved of Christian creeds, and likely the oldest, is the Apostles' Creed. A central component of its affirmations of faith is this: "I believe in the Holy Spirit, the holy catholic church, the communion of saints." Note that the church is pictured as an organic reality, a living organism growing out of prior belief and life in the Holy Spirit. The church is the house of true faith that is filled with the true believers, not an established religious institution.

The church is holy when it is catholic and a communion of saints, that is, when it is viewed as all of God's people and when God's people are committed to active and constructive relationships among themselves. The Holy Spirit births the church—which then is its true self only when exercising properly. What are the proper exercises? They are staying rooted in the Spirit's life and ministry (believing in the Holy Spirit), reaching hands of fellowship to all who are washed by the blood of the Lamb (Catholic), and being proactive about enriching and being enriched by all of God's children (the community of the saints).

Making Room for Others

Hospitality is another way of describing the will of a believer to keep open the revelation and spiritual-growth windows. Reaching graciously and listening carefully are essential exercises of being truly Christian. To be *holy* is to be *hospitable*. To be one with God is necessarily to be one with God's people and creation, loving and caring for them in all ways possible.

The people of ancient Israel knew well that they had been strangers and aliens who were graciously given an undeserved home by God—a promised land. Returning this unmerited favor to the vulnerable in their midst was part of what it meant for them to be the people of God acting like God. Jesus urged human hosts to open their banquet tables to more than the family and friends who could return the favor (Luke 14:12-14). The alienated Zacchaeus was "up a tree," likely less because he was short and more because he was not welcome on the ground with the others. Jesus noticed, stopped, and honored even this treed "stranger" (Luke 19:2-5).

Forgiveness opens the way to love. We become able to love others because of our experience of God's love for us (1 John 4:19). One of the great novels and musicals of recent times is *Les Misérables*. The central character, Valjean, receives a shocking gift from a bishop that sets the direction of his future life. A convicted thief becomes a selfless servant of others. Valjean shows profound Christian love after being set free from his old life by an act of sheer grace on his behalf. Forgiveness led to love, selfless relationships, and we might say to holiness. Once love takes root in the heart, the other Christian virtues (the "fruit of the Spirit") naturally grow.

> *How can the church overcome the deadening gravity, the weight of sin and self-centeredness, the bureaucracy and institutionalism of its sometimes obsolete structures? There is a way, the only way—it is inhaling the life-giving and life-sustaining breath of the Spirit of God (John 3:8), the flame of love that burns the false, generates the pure, and builds true community.*

Holiness is not a sacred doctrine to be locked in a closet and enjoyed only by an elite few who have the mysterious key. It is something to be treasured and lived by all believers as a love relationship with God in Jesus Christ through the Spirit. Holiness is *community* with God and then with each other in a transformed and loving fellowship we call the church.

Here is the right question and the only adequate answer. How can the church overcome the deadening gravity, the weight of sin, self-centeredness, bureaucracy and institutionalism of its sometimes obsolete structures? There is a way, the only way—it is inhaling the life-giving and life-sustaining breath of the Spirit of God (John 3:8), the flame of love that burns the false, generates the pure, and builds community.

The effectiveness of church life does not depend finally on human abilities and the quality of church programming; it rests on the power of God at work in the church's life (Zech. 4:6). The church "rides the wind of God's Spirit like a hawk endlessly and effortlessly circling and gliding in the summer sky. It ever pauses to wait for impulses of power to carry it forward to the nations.... [The] Spirit indwells the church as a perpetual Pentecost."[62] The Spirit works in and through healed and healing fellowships of believers who are consciously inhaling the new life and are truly open to others.

We need not—must not—choose between *God's agency* and *human practices* of spiritual growth. In fact, certain God-ordained practices are standard means of God's action (see chapter 9). The Spirit forms holy communities that grow in group holiness as the members engage faithfully in practices that God has chosen for serving well as channels of holy formation. Holy communities are the result, and they become capable of fostering the presence of love that reaches out to build and extend the community of faith. The house of God generates houses of God.

Here is another key question. How much room is made for others in the circle of divine grace, even for those not associated with Christianity as a formalized religion? This is an increasingly urgent question in our shrinking world where all faith communities are becoming close neighbors. Here is the biblical answer: God appears to be the great lover of lost humanity, desiring that *all* be saved (1 Tim. 2:4). God is open to all people; in God's name, we must be also.

Some of us believe wrongly that the saved will be just our group, nation, or community of correct belief. But God is the Father of all, extends his loving heart toward all, had all in mind when Jesus was on that cross, and sent his Spirit "who can foster transforming friendships with God anywhere and everywhere."[63] God leaves a witness everywhere, even though the clearest witness has appeared in one human life—Jesus. Our instinct is to close the windows of religion's house and control carefully the membership list of the righteous. An important holy exercise is to keep making room for all of God's children, allowing the Judge of the ages to distinguish where we cannot.

Monasticism has long tried to carry the Christian call to hospitality, balancing holiness as *separation* from the world with holiness as a radical *openness* to the world. For many years I have been privileged to do spiritual retreats at the historic Gethsemani monastery in Kentucky. There are high walls there, yes, and deliberate differences from "the world." There also is a gracious ministry of hospitality that has taken me in rather than turning me away. I am a Protestant seeking deeper roots and a wider reach.

Where is the boundary between the called and saved and those who are not? That is a decision of the Spirit, not ours—fortunately since my ability (and yours) to judge others properly is so limited. Our spiritual exercise plan calls for keeping windows open and extra rooms available for unexpected guests.

One contemporary Catholic priest testifies that his holiness journey has made him a believer without a country "and yet a man who could go to any country and be at home." He has learned to "puddle-jump between countries, cultures, and concepts…being moved toward a greater inclusivity in my ideas, a deeper understanding of people, and a more honest sense of justice." God has given him a bigger heart and has led him to more distant places.

This brother has grasped an important part of the Christian faith. While faithful to a particular order of his Roman Catholic tradition, he has learned that the house of faith is larger than many of us recognize. So, he concludes, "I finally had to be either *Roman* or *catholic*, and I continue to choose the *catholic* end of that spectrum."[64] Similarly, I continue to be a Protestant, but one ready to "protest" the shortcomings that occur at home as well as elsewhere. I belong to the whole church, and in Christ it all belongs to me!

The house of Christian faith is surrounded by the homeless and helpless, immigrants, refugees, orphans, and other strangers—this world is hardly the best of neighborhoods. To be holy in this house is to have the windows open, with welcoming hands outstretched. Note this disturbing reality:

> We, like the early church, find ourselves in a fragmented and multicultural society that yearns for relationships, identity, and meaning. Our mobile and self-oriented society is characterized by disturbing levels of loneliness, alienation, and estrangement…. People are hungry for welcome but most Christians have lost track of the heritage of hospitality.[65]

This irony must change. To be holy is to be actively exercising hospitality. Paul says that we are to be "given to hospitality" (Rom. 12:13). In our kind of world, to reach out is risky, costly, subversive, living from a different, a holy, a biblical value system, marching to a drummer that even many "religious" people do not seem to hear. No matter. To live otherwise is to not be one with Jesus. It is to be breathing air that is not the Spirit's!

LIVING IN THE RIGHT HOUSE

Staying *In* by Going *Out*

Being inside the Christ house is certainly a precious privilege, a gift of grace, an amazing opportunity to rejoice and grow. We must never forget, however, that entering the "holy of holies" is also fraught with dangers. The windows can get shut—our defensive action that blunts the free flowing of God's Spirit of ever-fresh divine air. The "Welcome" sign can get replaced with "Enter the secret code and press pound."

How easy it is to think that we are the only apple of God's eye, that we have it all right and are clearly holier than those who are knocking on the door, needing in. When we do not understand their languages and experiences and they do not belong to our tribe, nation, race, or denomination, we tend to find ways to exclude. Doing God's business comes to be little more than trying to duplicate our own likeness and claiming certainty that all is authorized by God exactly as we are understanding and practicing it.

Holiness people have been known to install an internal security system in Christ's house that fails to make room for others who wish to enter, even those who may be invited and motivated by God. Once inside, there is a tendency to become withdrawn in our little religious cocoons. Rather than emerging as beautiful butterflies, we feel safer, even holier when we remain sealed—eventually dying right in the courts of God!

John Wesley has good advice here. Holiness is healthy only when exercised in acts of mercy. To be holy is hardly to be a polished statue smiling high above the world's pain. To be holy is to be reaching out to the hurting, being hospitable to them. Yes, we are to "evangelize" them, but we are to do so by being God's agents of healing and justice. To insult the dignity of others or to ignore their physical as well as spiritual needs is to violate God's way of spreading the good news of Jesus. The best way to stay in God's righteous house is to go outside on missions of mercy.

There is a deep irony that injures God's work and fouls the air inside his house. It is simply this: There is a *going out* required if one is to *stay in*. Although Wesley had others in mind when he said the following in his tract *Character of a Methodist*, it applies to all followers of Jesus, all of today's residents of God's holy house:

> A Methodist is one who has "the love of God shed abroad in his heart by the Holy Ghost given to him"; one who "loves the Lord his God with all his heart, and with all his soul, and with all his mind, and with all his strength...." He "does good unto all men"—unto neighbours, and strangers, friends, and enemies. And that in every possible kind; not only to their bodies, by "feeding the hungry, clothing the naked, visiting those that are sick or in prison," but much more does he labour to do good to their souls.

Therefore, being holy in God's house requires keeping the windows open, hanging out the welcome sign for strangers, and leaving regularly to go and do acts of mercy in the name of the owner of the house. All of this is great, grace-full, holy exercise. It is breathing actively the very breath of God.

CHAPTER 9

EXERCISING THE "MEANS" OF GRACE

Therefore prepare your minds for action; discipline yourselves.... Like obedient children, do not be conformed to the desires that you formerly had in ignorance. Instead, as he who called you is holy, be holy yourselves in all your conduct (1 Peter 1:13-15).

Train yourself in godliness for, while physical training is of some value, godliness is valuable in every way (1 Tim. 4:7-8).

How do we move forward in holiness? We train for lives of holiness, "we undertake activities of body, mind and spirit that in time will build spiritual resources within us to act appropriately when the situation demands it. As athletes of God, we plan a regimen of spiritual disciplines that will stimulate our growth in grace."[66] We exhale death and inhale life.

The above quotes set the stage well. The holy life is not gained or sustained without disciplined effort. Believers need to exercise means of spiritual growth, some of which are especially established by God for this purpose. But an initial word of caution is in order.

All grace-full means for spiritual growth have a major limitation. They are not magical—no one goes through the right motions with the automatic result of a matured holiness. The "means" are crucial, even God-given, but they are worthless apart from proper motivation for their use and the present ministry of the Spirit of God. The motions of God-likeness lack value without the breath of God enlivening them in us.

Spiritual Growth Hormones

Physical and spiritual exercises are similar in several ways. For instance, there is a correlation between lack of exercise and the presence of anxiety. During exercise, the body releases endorphins that encourage feelings of well being. During spiritual exercise, the Spirit releases growth hormones that stimulate holiness characteristics—real, not only felt.

Spiritual growth is much like popular dieting and exercise programs. They can be effective or mere fads. When well-chosen exercises are included as a regular part of life, God's goals for his children are achieved. When they are not taken seriously and used with disciplined regularity, life becomes stunted and may even decay. Nothing works unless actually used with the right attitudes and goals and pursued persistently. And we can be assured of this. God has not left us without tools for the task. There are proven standards for and effective means of spiritual growth for Christians. We must know and use them well.

There also are cautions and ironies related to all spiritual exercise programs. Here is one crucial guideline, really a paradox. Spiritual growth is a community affair—believers need each other as they grow; they also need room for their own personal individuality. We must do this together, and yet we must not think that growth happens in exactly the same ways for everyone or that the goal is that we will all look, act, and think alike when we have become mature—holy.

The church can—and must—"affirm individual dignity...without enshrining individualism. It can realize community without authorizing lordship or establishment."[67] Jesus chose to serve by giving his life, not calling on the available twelve legions of angels to force his will on anyone (Matt. 26:53). One thing we humans must exercise with wisdom and discipline is the freedom of choice that God has given—but without ever deciding to go it alone.

The goal of Christian spiritual growth (sanctification) is a believer's transformation into what C. S. Lewis once called "little Christs." We are to be transformed into the likeness of Jesus "until Christ is formed in you" (Gal. 4:19). To be "holy" is to be more than forgiven of sin. It is to gain possession of Christ-like character, be filled with Christ-breath, and then act accordingly. Holiness is the restoration of God's image in us. Jesus, the perfect expression of the divine in the human, is our model and goal. His Spirit is our dynamic.

What a goal! How do we get there? It will not be sudden or automatic. It will not be separate from life with God's people. It always will require the growth hormones and fresh air that only the Spirit dispenses and as we release by exercising properly. We must employ every means available, and do so reverently, with discipline, over time, and together.

> *There is no need to reinvent the wheel. Spiritually sensitive Christians have been trying to show the way for many centuries. We should learn from the church of all times. It is our cheering section, our great cloud of encouraging witnesses (Heb. 12:1), our supporting sisters and brothers, our company of spiritual growth instructors.*

Avoiding Protestant Paranoia

Let's be clear about one thing. We do not ever *achieve* this goal of Christ likeness, as though it were in our human power to do so. Gaining holiness is always a matter of God's grace. That being said, we nonetheless are called to be partners in the holiness-gaining process. So, what is the "how" of being effective partners with God?

There is no need to reinvent the wheel. Spiritually sensitive Christians have been trying to show the way for many centuries. We should learn from the church of all times. It is our cheering section, our great cloud of encouraging witnesses (Heb. 12:1), our supporting sisters and brothers, our company of spiritual growth instructors. We can learn from those who have gone this way before.

The word "Protestant" must not be allowed to mean that non-Catholics so protest the downsides of the church's past and present life that they miss the treasures of its rich tradition and continuing potential. There must be no "Protestant paranoia." By this I mean the fearing of church establishment so much that we fail to avail ourselves of the perennial "means" that God has provided for spiritual growth through the community of faith. It is true that God's grace and our proper responses should not—cannot—be captured in human boxes, institutionalized, standardized. Even so, a healthy and growing spiritual life necessarily involves "practices" designed to assist. Here is wisdom:

> By practices we mean doable habits or rhythms that transform us, rewiring our brains, restoring our inner ecology, renovating our inner architecture, expanding our capacities. We mean actions within our power that help us become capable of things currently beyond our power.[68]

I am in agreement with John Wesley on the subject of divine-human partnership. We believers are to be active in our seeking after the grace of God.

EXERCISING THE "MEANS" OF GRACE

A standard good-sense rule is this: One usually does not obtain a goal without employing the available means to get to that goal. We cannot do anything to force God to love, redeem, or sustain us. God is God. Our activity on behalf of spiritual growth is based on our belief that there exist certain actions that God has ordained as "ordinary" channels through which sanctifying grace will flow—*if* they are exercised by us humbly and in faith and in oneness with God's people.

These ordained actions are potentially "sacramental," that is, concrete actions that can become channels of divine grace stimulating spiritual growth. Despite the many "high-church" meanings attached to this word, sacramental simply means the sacred coming to us humans by way of material things or particular actions. The prime example is Jesus himself, God coming to us in human flesh ("incarnation"). Such enfleshing was capable of conveying saving grace; however, for us, we engage in sacraments not to receive saving but *maturing* grace, and this is the case *only if* we actors practice them for the right reasons and with the right motivations.

Here is an important definition that some Protestants fail to follow. Christian life is striving to become oriented away from self-absorption and toward the eternal life with and for God. Because such new life comes only from God, it is known to be a gift of divine grace. However, because this gift is never automatic or coerced, there necessarily is to be *a striving toward its attainment.* No one can create or earn eternal life, but we can and must do one very important thing. We can and must choose to act in ways that place us in the best position to receive God's grace gifts for growth. God is resourceful and faithful, the redemption initiator; much beyond that depends on us.

While God makes it possible for all believers to travel the road to "perfection," we must decide to take the journey. And we must remember that "spiritual perfection" is not flawless performance of God's will in this world—something that sin has put beyond us for now. Sanctification is a wholeness of renewed relationship with God out of which we choose to do God's will in every way we know and that our limitations will allow. "Perfection" is a *relational* term; the goal is renewed relationship with our loving and redeeming God.

> *There is a hurtful Protestant paranoia, the inordinate fear of "works righteousness." If salvation does not come because of our "works," we sometimes think, then we dare not work in the process of its coming, risking the impression that we are earning what only God's grace provides. The fact is, however, that we can honor God's grace provision so highly that we spoil its potential in our lives by our own neglect of doing what we can and honoring both the individual and the community of faith in the process.*

Holiness involves intentional action, practicing disciplined love that builds up personal life and the fellowship of believers. Peter instructs believers to purify their souls "by obedience to the truth" for the holy purpose of "genuine mutual love." Therefore, "love one another deeply from the heart" (1 Peter 1:22). Practicing holiness involves active lives of neighborly love. "Above all," says Peter, "maintain constant love for one another, for love covers a multitude of sins" (4:8). When it comes to selfless love, exercise often and well!

What should we be doing? Protestants must be doing more than protesting the failures of others. Peter says that we are to prepare our minds for action through the disciplining of ourselves. What might this discipline look like? He goes into detail, insisting that his readers had lived long enough in the lifestyle of the Gentiles and now needed to exchange living by their human desires for living by the will of God (1 Peter 4:1-6)—including lives of prayer, constant love, the showing of hospitality, and serving human needs as they are found.

EXERCISING THE "MEANS" OF GRACE

Doing such things well will involve reaching to the tradition (collected wisdom) of the whole church. The Eastern or Orthodox churches, for instance, stress healing as an imagery for holiness. God-ordained actions can be therapeutic, empowering our recovery of lost holiness. God is the healer; our appropriate actions help activate the healing of our souls. The Roman Catholic Church stresses particular God-ordained actions and tries to ensure by church control that they are properly understood and practiced. There is wisdom and danger in such control. Wise believers will be "Catholic" and "Protestant" and "Orthodox" as they exercise. We must be whole-church believers.

Protestant churches tend to resist church control, seeing it as excessive power and arrogance in church life. Catholics are believed to grant "tradition" too great a role. Protestants focus instead on the authority of biblical revelation, the present ministering of the Spirit of God, and a believer's deliberate walking with Christ in the power of his resurrection. They insist that Christ wants the church to be free of kings, legislatures, choking denominational structures, priests, official liturgies, and human lords of all kinds. All of these Christian traditions have their wisdoms and weaknesses. Protestants are correct, but not altogether.

I write as a Protestant, but one enriched by life in a particular Roman Catholic monastery (Gethsemani). I believe deeply in divine grace—we are saved *only* by God's gracious provisions in Christ. Still, there is a hurtful Protestant paranoia, the inordinate fear of "works righteousness." If salvation does not come because of our "works," we sometimes think, then we dare not work in the process of its coming, risking the impression that we are *earning* what only God's grace provides. The fact is, however, that we can honor God's grace provision so highly that we spoil its potential in our lives by our own neglect of doing what we can and honoring both the individual and the community of faith in the process.

We must act responsibly on what we know to do, always knowing that the holy healing depends ultimately on *what God does*. Soul healing or holiness regained certainly has a point of beginning—new life begun. But it also is a process with many stages of growth, and they are dependent in part on disciplines of life and faith that keep opening doors of increased potential. Holiness is not an instant and completed gift, nor is it only a process or an unreachable ideal.

True transformation is what is in view, the actual reshaping of our "affections" and the redirecting of our wills and attitudes. Holiness is being re-formed into the image of Jesus Christ, and there are particular exercises that can help get it done. James Earl Massey put it well: "The noblest work of Christ is shaping Christian character. It is his desire to confirm us in his pattern and spirit of life.... The disciplines that we assume can bless our will and give it moral constancy to remain habitually directed to what we see in Christ."[69]

What Are the "Means"?

If divine grace and human partnership are both involved in the gaining of Christian holiness, what specific exercises, what actions and disciplines on our part are we talking about? The answer is not entirely the same for all Christians. People go into a wellness center and have different workout needs and plans. Some run, some lift weights, some swim, with most having combinations of activities that best fit their physical circumstances and goals. Likewise, we must be careful not to overly standardize spirituality.

Holiness is impossible without the work of the Spirit of God, but the Spirit chooses not to sanctify us without cooperation. The Christian life is, from beginning to end a work of grace, and yet spiritual progress comes through a diligent exercise of the means of grace. If we follow the directions given by Christ himself, several action-disciplines appear central, normal, and are based on the following assumption about exercising for holiness.

Let's identify particular spiritual exercises, means of grace that foster mutual love and stimulate spiritual growth and self-less service to

EXERCISING THE "MEANS" OF GRACE

humankind—building blocks of holiness. The Christian faith community over the centuries has determined that the following four are especially biblical and crucial. Every spiritual exercise plan should include at least these. To do these humbly is to breath in the very breath and life of God.

1. **Living in the Word.** One essential exercise is living in God's revealed Word, regularly reading and absorbing the teachings found in the sacred Scripture of the Judeo-Christian tradition. This Bible reading and reflecting is to be done less for gaining religious information so that we can out-argue the uninitiated or win a Bible quiz or build an encyclopedia of sermons. Serious Bible reading is to be done more for experiencing personal transformation, the renewal of our characters, attitudes, motivations, and commitments. In the written Word (Bible) we come into contact with the Living Word (the Spirit of Christ), God now active in changing us into true words that God wants to speak to the world through us. Therefore, exercise your reading skills, thus stimulating your needed spiritual growth and sharpening the word you are to be for the world.

2. **Washing Properly.** A second essential exercise is public declaration of commitment to the lordship of Jesus Christ and oneness with God's people—baptism. We should wash properly and publically. The Lord himself modeled the baptismal act, signaling for us an important public washing and testimony. This exercise is our deliberate identifying with the cleansing grace of God and with the community of God's washed ones in this world. Baptism is far more than the physical act itself, or exactly how it is done. Insisting on particular mechanics of this exercise can distract from its central meaning and may cause some not to do it at all. It is the public witness itself

that strengthens both the one witnessing and the community of faith that receives the witness.

The crucial question is "not whether one had [has] been baptized, but whether one [is] continuing to participate responsibly in the transformation of life that the grace signified in baptism empowers."[70] The sanctifying good news is that, when we participate responsibly as God directs, we become increasingly able to participate fruitfully! Doing holiness exercises brings holiness results. Live in the Word. Be washed in the water.

3. **Eating with Jesus**. A third essential exercise is regular partaking of the Meal of Jesus or the Lord's Supper. The Lord spread a table of sacred symbols and called on his disciples to eat. Jesus said that we should do this often and together in remembrance of him (1 Cor. 11:24). Ingesting reverently in remembrance of the death and resurrection of Jesus nourishes spiritual growth. Exercising loyalty to the sharing of this meal involves two things: It enlivens memory and expands spiritual life by (1) re-presenting the sacrificial work of Christ on the cross, and (2) newly activating in the faithful participant an awareness and acceptance of the current presence of the sanctifying power of that saving work. Read, wash, and eat. See below for more on this eating.

4. **Praying Constantly**. Immersing ourselves in God's Word, proclaiming through baptism our oneness with God's people and mission, and eating together the sacred meal of Jesus are practices (exercises) always to be bathed with prayer. We all know the Lord's Prayer—Jesus has told us what to seek and with what attitudes we should ask.[71] Apparently, by Jesus'

personal example and specific instruction, his disciples then and now are to be people of constant prayer. Why? Prayer is a natural tool of relationship building. Prayer is the spiritual breathing that sustains our life in Christ.

All good spiritual activities involve a disciplined Spirit-breathing. The Christian life is to be lived in relationship to God, and prayer is a chief means of sustaining that relationship. It is the sacred conversation of exhaling and inhaling, releasing our own thoughts and concerns and praises toward God and then being silent so that we can receive back that which God has just for us. So, read, wash, eat, and always pray.

A New Monasticism?

Are the sanctifying actions, the holy breathing exercises, limited to the Word, baptism, the meal, and prayer? No. Other spiritual exercises are helpful. Different Christian communities tend to evolve specific traditions aimed at helping the process of the sanctification of believers (see the next chapter).

A prominent example is the *Rule of Saint Benedict* that has proven its value over many centuries. It has been the guide for a large portion of the monastic tradition of Christianity. At the heart of this Rule is practical guidance for leading simple lives of prayer and work. Also of prominent historical note is Ignatius Loyola who underwent a profound spiritual crisis that led to his founding one of the great missionary movements in Christian church history, the Jesuits. His best-known writing is *Spiritual Exercises* (1548). He knew that the attention of young believers had to be directed for their maximum spiritual benefit.

Obviously, most Christians today are not and cannot be living as monks. Even so, many are looking for the experience of being part of some disciplined Christian community, maybe like the "Holy Club" or "class meetings" of early Methodism.[72] There is today a "new monasticism," a fresh holiness movement springing up to serve busy modern Christians who long for more than church services scheduled when they have a little time between crowded commuter rides, fluctuating stock markets, ringing cell phones, and endless advertising grabbing for their attention.[73]

One exercise highlighted in the Wesleyan tradition appears essential. John Wesley insisted that the only true Christian holiness is a *social* holiness. That means at least two things. First, Christians mature best *together*—church relationships are important. The church is the scene where communion, baptism, and proclamation of the Word occur. These are community events and spiritual disciplines, necessary exercises for growth. Second, to become *like Christ* must involve *being Christ* to others. There is no deepening of Christian love in our lives unless there is an expressing of that love on behalf of the needs of others. Becoming mature in Christ is necessarily to be on mission for Christ, going arm-in-arm with fellow believers to hold the hands of the weak and hopeless.

We will *have* only what we are prepared to *enhance* and *give away*. The Hebrew heritage of Christianity makes clear that authentic religion is far more than a system of ethics, a code of conduct, or a creed, "orthodox" as all of these may be. True faith—actual holiness—involves how a person walks daily in light of belief in the ever-present God. Those who please God are those who are acting justly, loving mercy, and walking humbly with God (Micah 6:8). Therefore, "the essence of religion is relationship; it is walking with God in his path of wisdom and righteousness and in his way of service to others."[74] So, read, wash, eat, always pray, and actively minister.

There are many "means of grace," multiple spiritual exercises that can help reshape us into Christ's image and commission us into Christ's service. They tend to put us in a good position for such reshaping to occur by God's responding action. In the Wesleyan tradition, these exercises sometimes have been put into the categories of "works of piety" and "works of mercy." The first is oriented toward enhancing the love of God in our personal lives; the second looks to sharing the love in God with our neighbors in need. They all might be called *holy habits*. As they are exercised and ingrained in us, they become effective channels for receiving and expressing sanctifying grace.

True monasticism has less to do with walls around us and much more to do with finding ways to focus on the great challenge before us as believers. As divine grace flows through the several exercise channels, our very souls are healed and grow strong in the faith. We become Christ-like, fulfilling the vision of St. Paul that "all of us, with unveiled faces, seeing the glory of the Lord as though reflected in a mirror, are being transformed into the same image from one degree of glory to another; for this comes from the Lord, the Spirit" (2 Cor. 3:18).

Milestones of Progress

How do we know when the breathing of our spirits and the exercises of our bodies are being effective for our spiritual growth needs? What are the signs of the presence of true holiness?

Even though I am a theologian, I must say this: "Orthodox" theology is important—a strong body needs a sturdy bone structure that allows all normal movements and healthy exercises. But more than good theology

> *The signs of real spiritual progress include right remembering, participating in what is remembered, discerning Christ's body, and gladly accepting the risks and receiving the joys of living as new creations in the midst of this yet-old world. The result is "purity of heart," becoming a believer in whom the love of God has taken control. Our breath becomes God's breath; our human will begins to desire what God desires and willingly risk on behalf of what God intends.*

is important for Christian holiness. Following Jesus faithfully must bring particular life results that are quite noticeable to others. A mature (holy) Christian should evidence some distinguishing characteristics beyond good theological thinking. Walking in companionship with Jesus as his dedicated disciples should inspire lives that increasingly breathe and act like him.

What are the sure signs of spiritual progress, the proper outcomes of benefitting from the available means of grace? Sometimes the signs are called Christian "virtues." They are referred to in the New Testament as "fruit" of the Spirit. They are the visible substance of Christian character, the central characteristics of Christian maturity. A tree is known by its fruit. So are Christians.

Three holy character traits should come from faithful participation in the Lord's Supper—one of the essential spiritual exercises we identified above. When we participate deeply, truly, and often, these characteristics should come to be part of who we are and how we are in the world. The Lord's Supper is . . .

1. A *sanctifying* meal. This meal is a series of remembrance symbols. To remember in the biblical sense is to become vitally involved in the reality of what is remembered. This should be so much the case that Christ's death and resurrection story becomes the shaping power of our present life, of our personal stories. To be holy is to have obviously benefitted from Christ's sacrificial death by becoming like Christ in his servant life through the power of his resurrection.

2. A *social* meal. There is to be no more Jew/Greek, slave/free, or male/female discriminations in the church of Jesus (Gal. 3:28). To be holy involves dramatic social implications that emerge from being Christ-like. Part of the fruit of the Spirit

is "discerning the body" when we eat and drink at the Lord's table. We see and gladly affirm all who choose to eat with us, past and present, in our land and far away, of our color and culture and of others. To be holy is to be engaging in the righting of relationships and the forming of a new and inclusive community like the world does not know. To be sanctified is to be distinctively social in the radical way of Jesus. If any person belongs to Jesus by grace, that person is my brother or sister in grace. Here is a radical new way of being.

3. A *seditious* meal. To be in Christ and part of the Christ community at the table is to participate in a new creation. This fresh reality is the antithesis of the values, structures, and dynamics of the fallen world. To sit at the table with Christ is to declare one's ultimate allegiance to Christ, joining his spiritual force that is working within the world to undermine and renew it. To be holy is to deliberately hold membership in a higher order. It is to pledge allegiance to the King who is above all kings. It is to be faithful, whatever the cost, to the kingdom coming in Christ to reign over all of the human kingdoms. Love one's country, yes; love God's kingdom even more, yes!

The signs of real spiritual progress include right remembering, participating in what is remembered, discerning Christ's body, and gladly accepting the risks and receiving the joys of living as new creations in the midst of this yet-old world. The result is "purity of heart," becoming a believer in whom the love of God has taken control. Our breath becomes God's breath; our human will begins to desire what God desires and willingly risk on behalf of what God intends.

Progress on the holiness journey is reflected in the fresh style of how we function with those around us. Henri Nouwen once worded well this

Christ-like way of being: "When we are securely rooted in personal intimacy with the source of life, it will be possible to remain flexible without being relativistic, convinced without being rigid, willing to confront without being offensive, gentle and forgiving without being soft, and true witnesses without being manipulative."[75] This is a wonderful description of Christian discipleship and evangelism—and true holiness.

The holy way of being and relating can be seen in the following four "Ps" that should come to characterize true living in Christ.

1. **Presence**. The spiritually mature Christian woman or man loves the Bible and readily studies it *in community*. The holy ones know their own limitations and their need for the wisdom of the whole body of Christ (past and present, the traditional and the contemporary). They are present regularly in the body's life, but they do not subscribe to any group agenda that tries to use the Bible for human goals—like proving that *we are right* over other believers, advancing ourselves at the expense of others. The ultimate reason that the spiritually mature (and the immature hoping for maturity) study Scripture is "to encounter the living God as he has revealed himself in Christ through the personal presence of the Holy Spirit."[76] We consciously exercise our presence to the body and our openness to the body's Spirit.

    Biblical texts may inform about many things, but their ultimate purpose is not to function as a database of religious information on virtually all subjects of current interest, religious and otherwise. These sacred texts intend primarily to transform readers into the image of Jesus Christ. The Spirit who once "inspired" (in-breathed) these texts now seeks to bring them to life in us with fresh meaning for our time and place—fresh divine breath for our lungs and insight for our minds.[77] Holy ones are welcoming both to this past and the present inspiration of the sacred text. They are active church members contributing to the body and serious listeners to the Spirit's voice through the Word. They are present to the people and present to the sacred text.

2. **Perspective.** No longer does the spiritually mature believer need to think in terms of yes-or-no on all religious matters. Paradox is the stuff of life and should be received as a friend.[78] People are not to be judged as either for me or against me. Churches are no longer to be evaluated as having all the truth or not, having ideal performance or not—after all, none do. When still spiritually immature, prior to being "sanctified," the unloving black-and-white mind has a serious flaw. It "compares, it competes, it conflicts, it conspires, it condemns, it cancels out any contrary evidence, and it then crucifies with impunity, [becoming] the source of most violence, which is invariably *sacralized* as good and necessary…to 'save souls for heaven.'"[79]

Today's world is burdened with rampant violence, which unfortunately is often religiously motivated. By sharp contrast, Jesus was always welcoming the outsider, the foreigner, the sinner, the wounded, the doubter. To use the language of Richard Rohr, Jesus was a "second-half-of-life" man who had the unenviable task of trying to teach and be understood by a largely "first-half-of-life" world. That is, Jesus was full of the love of God (holy) and acted out of that love in the face of the loveless, the unholy, many of whom were very "religious." He knew paradox and saw the larger picture. Such maturity rarely is seen in the young of age or in the disciple of any age who has not gained the broad perspective that comes only by "going on to perfection."

3. **Personality.** The spiritually mature are those who live and grow in the community of faith. While gladly a part of "body life," they nonetheless remain very much individuals. To be "sanctified" is to be a contributing member of a set-apart community, but it is not finally to conform to any rigid template of the perfect Christian as defined by any particular group of believers. Those living deeply in the love of God will always be distinct individuals with particular personalities, gifts, and callings (1 Cor. 12). While we will not all be eyes or ears of the one body, we all will gladly live and work interdependently. This is one of those paradoxes of Christian faith that must come to be accepted—we are *individuals* who belong *in community*, but without our distinctive selves becoming mere pawns of the community. Sadly, some communities of faith are highly dysfunctional, determined to get everyone "in line."

    Given communities of faith naturally develop their particular group personalities and cultures. Even so, churches should become holy, not just individual members. A truly Spirit-filled, holy community is characterized by "its supernatural ability to rise above the divisions and hostilities that characterize our world in order to live in it as a signpost of God's reign…. [For instance], the world is divided by race, ethnicity and nationality, but a holy community will strive to cross these boundaries by embracing believers 'from every nation, from all tribes and peoples and languages' (Rev. 7:9)."[80] They will cross boundaries in their distinctive ways relevant to their own settings—but they will do it with courage and to God's glory.

    All believers can be truly Christ-like without the violation of their individualities. We breathe the same Spirit-air and yet are individual instruments in the Spirit's hands.

4. **Patience.** Congregations and individual Christian believers living in a spiritually mature state of love must not expect that such maturity will always and quickly exist in others, especially in others outside the church. The necessary challenge is to exercise patience and learn to live lovingly among those less advanced in their faith journeys. People, and especially institutions, are usually programmed to function at a level below that of love. One must not expect of others what they are not yet able to give, getting frustrated and even angry in the process.

   One temptation that must be resisted is disrespecting and manipulating others who are not spiritually sensitive let alone mature. Those in an early stage of faith still struggle with issues of identity and boundary protection. They are still absorbed with themselves despite being forgiven sinners. Holiness will exhibit patience, loving patience with spiritually immature brothers and sisters. Refusing to do so is a sure sign that holiness is not as present as claimed.

We now have established that there are breathing and exercising groundrules to be followed by all believers at all times. They are necessary holiness signposts, non-negotiable rules of the spiritual road. Certain theological assumptions must be honored if spiritual exercising is to be constructive and not destroy or at least deflect God's highest intentions for our lives. Now we turn to a recognition that there are multiple ways of exercising and nourishing our divine gifts for maximum spiritual well being. Some have found entirely different spiritual traditions and others represent varying forms of standard exercises, such as we have identified in this chapter. Some are more effective for given believers than for others—it depends on a variety of factors.

CHAPTER 10

AVAILABLE BREATHING PLANS

When the day of Pentecost had come, they were all together in one place. And suddenly from heaven there came a sound like the rush of a violent wind.... All of them were filled with the Holy Spirit and began to speak in other languages, as the Spirit gave them ability (Acts 2:1-2, 4).

Today a mighty river of the Spirit is bursting forth from the hearts of women and men, boys and girls. It is a deep river of divine intimacy, a powerful river of holy living, a dancing river of jubilation in the Spirit, and a broad river of unconditional love for all peoples.... The astonishing new reality in this mighty flow of the Spirit is how sovereignly God is bringing together streams of life that have been isolated from one another for a very long time.... In reality these different Traditions describe various dimensions of the spiritual life.[81]

When you intentionally do things for your own soul's well being, you will begin to feel a river flowing within, a divine stream of expanding joy. It is time to get intentional. Make a plan. Start breathing with the Spirit and doing spiritual exercises. As you do, be aware of this: We each are different persons and remain individuals, even when committed to the faith community and the holiness journey. There is no standard plan recognized by all Christians for going on to Christian perfection (holiness). Therefore, at least to some degree, a program of spiritual breathing and exercising must be individualized.

Whatever the variables, there are available some standard responses to the grace of God that is reaching into our lives. They are particular Christian disciplines, ways of obediently exercising faith in Jesus Christ and keeping faith with the Spirit's desired work in us. These disciplines encourage in us the conditions that must be present if what is truly "Christian" is to be realized, sustained, and exhibited in daily life. They are ways of deliberately ordering the self and opening it to growth. Some particular grouping of these ways is best for you.

The believer seeking the fullness of Christian life must be the disciplined to follow the vision of holiness and discover that best grouping—which may change over time. The beginning is first to be set apart, "sanctified" by God's initiating and saving grace. The next is to be launched into the process of "being sanctified." Yes, the sanctified believer must go on being sanctified. The Christ who is accepted as Savior must also be welcomed "as a companioning presence...the indwelling Spirit who works with us, shaping our personal history in ever-expanding phases and stages."[82]

The Variety of Standard Streams

We have identified baptism and communion, the washing and the eating, as standard spiritual activities in the historic Christian community. Even so, there are variations in how each of these is understood and practiced among Christians. Varying traditions can bring richness or confusion. These variations sometimes have cultural origins and often come from particular readings of the Bible that get hardened (unfortunately) into fixed, exclusive, and mandatory church teaching and practice.

The spiritual practice of the Lord's Supper is a prime example. It is widely treasured among Christians. Even so, just recalling what this exercise is called by different Christians highlights the variety of its practice. We "take Communion" and/or "participate in the Lord's Supper" and/or "celebrate the Eucharist" as a memorial or a fresh sacrifice. Likewise, the virtually universal practice of baptism has its several differences that sometimes become divisive among believers. Who are proper candidates, adult believers only or even babies? How should the practice be implemented? Should the water be sprinkled, poured, or made so deep that the candidate can be fully immersed? On go the variations and each is very important to some Christian group.

The variety among Christians comes from more than different approaches to how to practice the standard spiritual exercises. There also are several approaches to the spiritual life as a whole that create differing sets of priorities and ways of reading the Bible. The Christian quest to interpret the faith and apply it properly to ever-changing circumstances has never ceased

> *In his classic book* Streams of Living Water, *Richard Foster identifies six rich streams of Christian spiritual tradition, each different in emphasis and yet all exhibiting important aspects of Christian faith and life. He argues convincingly that these streams, while often separated from each other by time and place, should flow together into the richness and wholeness of the one river of God (the "Mississippi of the Spirit").*

since the earthly time of Jesus—and it always seems to be introducing fresh variations.

In his classic book *Streams of Living Water*, Richard Foster identifies six rich streams of Christian spiritual tradition, each different in emphasis and yet all exhibiting important aspects of Christian faith and life. He argues convincingly that these streams, while often separated from each other by time and place, should flow together into the richness and wholeness of the one river of God (the "Mississippi of the Spirit").[83]

Christians individually and denominations corporately often are seriously out of balance, stressing one of these streams almost to the exclusion of the others. But, apart from the witness of all the streams, any believer or body of believers is stunted to some degree in spiritual growth and mission vision. To exclude is to silence the voice of other streams that belong to the church's past and are crucial for the fullness of its present and future.

Each of these streams is susceptible to perversion, of course, especially if it is isolated from the others. Each is a treasure of some biblical truth that must be honored and actively practiced as circumstances allow. Each originated with Jesus himself who embodied the full range of holy characteristics before they found their differing ways into the various historic traditions of Christianity.

To be holy in the fullest and best sense involves the exercise of drinking deeply from these several traditions, different as they may appear on the surface. Following are the six spiritual streams in brief. Each offers valuable insights, has had great models in church history, and can be furthered in your own life by the use of particular spiritual exercises encouraged by each.

1. **The Evangelical Stream.** This stream of Christian spirituality focuses on the lived witness and preached word of the good news of God in Jesus Christ. It has full trust in the biblical

AVAILABLE BREATHING PLANS

revelation and cares deeply about right doctrine arising from that revelation. This tradition addresses the crying need of lost sinners to hear good news proclaimed and see it lived so that conviction is generated, forgiveness is sought, and new life in Christ is received. Thus, evangelism is stressed.

Powerful preaching of the good news began soon after Pentecost when Peter proclaimed the life-changing meaning of Jesus (Acts 2:14-36). The response of those hearers? "What should we do?" Peter's answer was, "Repent and be baptized... so that your sins may be forgiven" (Acts 2:38). As Paul soon would put it: "In Christ God was reconciling the world to himself, not counting their trespasses against them, and entrusting the message of reconciliation to us. So we are ambassadors [evangels] for Christ since God is making his appeal through us" (2 Cor. 5:19-20).

Billy Graham has preached the Christian gospel with powerful conviction in more places and to more people than anyone else in history (see his 1997 autobiography *Just As I Am*). Other model appearances of this tradition include Martin Luther (d.1546), Charles Finney (d.1875), Dwight L. Moody (d.1899), John R. Mott (d.1955), and C. S. Lewis (d.1963).

Spiritual exercises for this tradition? A basic task highlighted is getting serious about Bible study and preaching. The written Word brings the good news and leads to conviction of sin and repentance through the ministry of the Holy Spirit. Then disciples should get to know the "unsaved," learning their languages, social settings, and felt needs. Such knowledge opens doors to gospel sharing. One warning is in order. Learn about the long teaching tradition of the church, not just the emphases of a home denomination. It is the biblical/

apostolic faith that is to be shared, not merely a given and relatively modern aspect of it.

2. **The Contemplative Stream.** This stream focuses on the prayer-filled life that seeks intimacy with God. Deep spiritual understanding comes through the contemplation of those whose hearts have been closely attuned to God. There is to be a centering on the human longing for the practice of the presence of God that yields wisdom and discernment coming directly from God. The psalmist often meditated on God's character, law, and creation. John, exiled on the Isle of Patmos, experienced profound visions of God's future as he meditated in prayer. We are told that there is to be found a "peace that passes understanding" (Phil. 4:7). The highest wisdom exceeds the capacity of mere words.

Evelyn Underhill (d.1941), Frank Laubach's life (d.1970) and classic book *Letters of a Modern Mystic*, and the many writings of Thomas Merton (d.1968) and Henri Nouwen (d.1996) illustrate well this tradition. All have emphasized that a loving attention to one's relationship with God and a growing union with God are essential to a healthy and satisfying Christian life.

Spiritual exercises for this tradition? A basic practice is the discipline of intense and extended prayer, often alone in one's "closet." Take a long walk. Find an isolated place and sit in silence. Open the Bible, read slowly, and expect to hear from God. Just abide. After all, "God is love, and those who abide in love abide in God, and God abides in them" (1 John 4:16). Obvious cautions are the potential loss of the community of faith and the risk of an excessive and unchecked inwardness of faith experience.

3. **The Holiness Stream.** This stream focuses on the inward re-formation of the heart and character by divine grace, and the development of "holy habits" that reflect Christ in one's attitudes and actions. This tradition (obviously central to this book) addresses the human longing for "entire sanctification," becoming one with God in newness of life. Its biblical base begins with our learning that we are to be holy as God is holy (Lev. 19:1-2).

   The Sermon on the Mount of Jesus is a dramatic call to such holiness. Peter reports that we are to become nothing less than "participants in the divine nature" (2 Peter 1:4). The book of James stresses being immersed in a new reality that produces a new kind of person—and thus a new kind of moral character and resulting actions. Holy habits tend to deepen into fixed moral patterns of Christ-like life. We become "perfected" into the persons God originally created us to be.

   John Wesley (d.1791), Phoebe Palmer (d.1874), E. Stanley Jones (d.1973), and Dietrich Bonhoeffer (d.1945) well illustrated this

> *The six spiritual streams of Christianity are not mutually exclusive. They overlap, are parts of one whole. Each is valuable, biblical, worthy of present application in the life of every Christian. No one stream is adequate when separated from the others. All are to be exercised in the path to and resulting life of holiness. Believers differ by being immersed mostly in one stream, but we all should exercise the will to grow by widening our appreciation for spiritual streams not yet emphasized in our own experience.*

tradition. Bonhoeffer was martyred in part for attacking "cheap grace"—grace without discipline and costly discipleship is not true Christianity. The moral vision of Jesus' Sermon on the Mount must not be reduced to an impossible ideal. Jesus and later Bonhoeffer called the church to dare *being* the church, something that is different from this fallen world and sometimes is dangerous—they were both executed. Wesley called for a "going on to perfection," being genuinely changed.

Spiritual exercises for this tradition? We have identified above several "means of grace," particular actions one should take to stimulate spiritual growth and strength. Take them seriously. Beyond being forgiven by Christ, determine to become Christ-like through humble life in Christ's Spirit. Be active by engaging in "works of mercy."

4. **The Charismatic Stream**. This stream focuses on the empowering gifts of God's Spirit for spiritual growth and effective service. This tradition addresses the deep yearning for experiencing the immediacy of God's presence and work among his people. The Apostle Paul was set apart by the Spirit (Acts 13:2), and sent out by the Spirit (Acts 13:4), all after being filled by the Spirit (Acts 13:9). In 1 Corinthians he gives wise instruction on how to exercise spiritual gifts so that the result is for the good of the church. The problem is that spiritual gifts can be abused, becoming little more than self-oriented "enthusiasms."

    Because of the large subjective dimension, this stream often has been both praised and criticized. With proper cautions in place, however, this stream remains crucial for Christians. The Spirit blows wherever and however it chooses (John 3:8) and will never be domesticated. So, "be filled with the Spirit as you sing psalms and hymns and spiritual songs among yourselves, singing and making melody to the Lord in your hearts" (Eph. 5:18b-19).

Francis of Assisi (d.1226), George Fox (d.1691), William Seymour (d.1922), and John Wimber (d.1997) well illustrated this tradition, even if in various ways and in very different times and settings. This also was true of Clark Pinnock (d.2010), a classic "evangelical" with clear charismatic leanings.[84]

Spiritual exercises for this tradition? The Charismatic stream reminds believers that the kingdom of God "depends not on talk but on power" (1 Cor. 4:20). Believers should practice openness to God's presence, gifting, and empowering. They should rejoice in the immediacy of the Spirit's presence and work. Each believer should receive and become an active instrument of God's Spirit.

5. **The Social Justice Stream.** This stream focuses on the need for showing mercy and working for justice in all social relationships and structures. Said the ancient prophet, "Let justice roll down like waters, and righteousness like an ever-flowing stream" (Amos 5:24). This tradition addresses the gospel imperative for equity and compassion for all people in all settings. These are to be inevitable outcomes of authentic faith. To be holy requires actively serving God's people in this troubled world.

John Wesley said that there is no holiness but *social* holiness. Being intimate with God and coming alive in God's Spirit, although foundational, are not to be isolated selfish experiences. They are to be enfleshed by practical application to the urgent needs of today's people and the social systems in which they struggle to live.

John Woolman (d.1772), William Booth (d.1912), Dorothy Day (d.1980), Mother Teresa (d.1997), and Martin Luther King, Jr. (d.1968) have exhibited well the heart of this spiritual stream. Believers must practice in public what they preach—sometimes at a high personal price.

Spiritual exercises for this tradition? Recognize that Christian spirituality should relate to more than inward "experiences." The faith is called to reach outward and have very practical applications that impact the many injustices of this world. Ask these questions of yourself. What degrades the lives of people around you? What can be done to change the wrong? Christ overturned tables that were making a mockery of God's house. What should you be overturning in his name? Practice justice and exercise equity.

6. **The Incarnational Stream.** This stream focuses on making present and visible in the particulars of ordinary life the realm of the invisible Spirit of God. It is concerned with the relationship of spirit and matter, faith and work. This tradition stresses a "sacramental" way of living (the divine life conveyed to believers through ordinary objects and practices) in which the presence and grace of God is found and applied in everyday life. Jesus was born in humble circumstances, led a simple life of bare essentials, and made God known to ordinary people by "incarnating" (enfleshing) the divine presence in the midst of our sordid world. We have unlimited opportunities to do the same in simple and yet profound ways. William Temple once wrote a famous chapter on the "sacramental universe" in *Nature, Man, and God* (first ed. 1934).

The Quakers represent one Christian body that has taken this concern seriously. Other appearances of this stream include Isaac Newton (d.1727), Susanna Wesley (d.1742), Samuel Johnson (d.1784), John Henry Newman (d.1890), and Dag Hammarskjöld (d.1961) who brought practical action into the international work of the United Nations.[85]

Spiritual exercises for this tradition? Take seriously the "ordinary time" of the Christian calendar, those months after the big Easter-Pentecost celebration when one must learn to live the life of faith in the typical days when trumpets are not blowing and crowds are not present. Note the passages of Scripture that are selected in the lectionaries for study during these weeks of the calendar. Join the concern for "ecology," becoming a better steward of this earth. Choose carefully what you consume, create, and throw away.

Note that these six spiritual streams of Christianity are not mutually exclusive. They overlap, are parts of one whole. Each is valuable, biblical, worthy of present application in the life of every Christian. No one stream is adequate when separated from the others. All are to be exercised in the path to, and resulting life of, holiness. Believers do and will differ by being immersed mostly in a given stream, but we all should exercise the will to grow by widening our appreciation for spiritual streams not yet emphasized in our own experience.

Recommendations of Spiritual Coaches

Having made clear that there are numerous variations in Christian judgments about the "best" spiritual exercise programs (no one size seems to fit all), allow me to mention a few of the numerous spiritual coaches available for our guidance. They have enriched Christians in recent decades as they have sought to sort through the options and make practical recommendations. No one has the final word, of course, but all of the following books contain very good first words. They are listed chronologically and in no order of priority.

1. D. Elton Trueblood, *The Essence of Spiritual Religion* (1936)
2. Richard Foster, *The Celebration of Discipline* (1978)
3. James Earl Massey, *Spiritual Disciplines* (1985)
4. Dallas Willard, *The Spirit of the Disciplines* (1988)
5. Joseph Driskill, *Protestant Spiritual Exercises* (1999)
6. Barry L. Callen, *Authentic Spirituality* (2006)
7. Elaine Heath and Scott Kisker, *Longing for Spring* (2010)
8. Don Thorsen and Barry L. Callen, *Heart and Life* (2012)

There are many great coaches (spiritual mentors), and also many valuable exercises recommended.

The following three exercises are beneficial spiritual efforts for every Christian believer, and each certainly has biblical roots and current relevance.

1. **Call Time Outs.** Here is an interesting fact: At least as much is said in the Bible about "fasting" as about giving. The missionary activity of the church began in Antioch when Barnabas and Saul were commissioned: "Then after fasting and praying they laid their hands on them and sent them off" (Acts 13:3).

    Praying as Jesus instructed is to include fasting. He assumed the discipline of fasting for himself and his first disciples, although being careful to point out both to its important potential and its considerable pitfalls (Matt. 6:16-18). There will be a rich reward if fasting is done in secret and for the right reasons, not as a pathetic public display of shallow piety—the reward of which is only passing public notice.

The point of proper fasting is not to look dismal and feel deprived. To the contrary, fasting as a Christian spiritual exercise can be a means of actually gathering spiritual resources. In the midst of the abstaining, fasting should be an act of *affirmation*. It is to be a positive way of waiting on God, a way that can induce within us an increased awareness of the spiritual dimension of life. Fasting is not a renunciation of life; it is a means by which new life can be released within us. It is a form of self-death resulting in a spiritual resurrection. As the Spirit gains possession of our attention and hearts, testimony is freshly received that we really are children of God (Rom. 8:16).

To "diet" is generally assumed to mean an unwelcome self-denial of the food we love. But fasting should not be viewed that way. It is not to be a demeaning of the body's needs. Nor should it be a fleeing from the world that God is calling us to enter with words and lives of good news. Instead, it should be a willing exhaling of the temporarily distracting so that we can be inhaling fresh winds of the Spirit. Here is the point: Fasting is an exercise that can intensify our spiritual attention and create an emptiness that then can be filled by the overshadowing of the Holy Spirit, who then brings about an increased fullness of Christ within. To avoid food temporarily can increase the effectiveness of deep spiritual breathing. To fast is a way to become full!

Jesus modeled this process in the wilderness (Matt. 4:1-11), after which he was "filled with the power of the Spirit, returned to Galilee, and a report about him spread through all the surrounding country" (Luke 4:14). When John was exiled in what was supposed to be a miserable solitude on the island of Patmos, God used the emptiness to fill John with wisdom and joy rarely known on the struggling human scene. Being "in the

Spirit" (Rev. 4:2), John was blessed with profound insight into the ways and intentions of God. The desert, the vacant space created by fasting, is a good place for serious dialogue with the Holy Spirit who makes the desert bloom with good news and inspired ministry (Isaiah 35:1).

In our consumer-oriented society, it may be a greater sacrifice for us to fast than to give. Fasting should involve more than the temporary restriction of food intake. How difficult would it be for you to turn off the television, computer screens, and smart phones for one week (even one day!) in favor of much more looking into the biblical text and more time for prayer? To what are we addicted, other than the presence, voice, and will of God? To find out, exercise the discipline of fasting. It is a way of focusing on God.

Let me be clear. Fasting is not an attempt to subtly manipulate God, but an intentional opening to the divine for divine purposes in our lives. It is a good way of allowing for an inner solitude. It routinely sets aside time and space for undivided attention to God's presence, purposes, and provisions. Exercise this spiritual discipline. Dare to call a time out!

2. **Have Many Meetings.** It may sound contradictory, but it is not. Having called a time out (fasted), now go ahead and arrange for many meetings! This is what Jesus often did. He slipped away to pray, and then he came right back to meet and teach the crowds. Most professional and church people are tired of constant meetings, I know. Spiritually speaking, however, our world is hungry for many more, at least more of the Jesus kind.

Martin Buber (d.1965) was a Jewish philosopher known for his distinction between *I–Thou* and *I–It* relationships, viewing another person as a genuine person to value (Thou) or a thing to use (It). All real living is "meeting," he insisted. To view another person as a thing makes true meetings impossible. Our human prejudices, racisms, nationalisms, and even formalized religions too often encourage us to make "things" of people who are unlike us.

Attitudes of condescension reduce the "unfit" to a status below ourselves, destroying dialogue, true meeting, and real conversation. We then talk *at*, not *with*, others. So, who are the holy people? They are the ones who are separated from the crowd by God and empowered by the Spirit to imitate Jesus by initiating many true and loving conversations. Being like Jesus transforms hostility into peace by true self-giving love expressed in vulnerable and redemptive exchanges with others.

Some Christian evangelists have been guilty of severe condescension, speaking sharply at "sinners" they do not know personally and demanding that they repent or else! There is no meeting, no person-to-person contact, and no I-Thou conversation in such speaking. There is mostly the threat of Hell if there is no agreement and repentance. By contrast, Jesus gave himself to a ministry of dialogue, treating even his opponents as persons of worth in God's eyes. They were worthy of his personal time. He took risks to be with them in serious conservation—tax collectors, prostitutes, Samaritans, people "good Jews" of his day avoided as unworthy, as "its." Jesus connected and spoke truth in love, always having proper regard for the person to whom he was speaking—and, of course, he was made to pay the ultimate price by the offended religious "establishment."

This *I-Thou* insight is central to who God is and how God chooses to relate to us humans, now a spoiled creation. The cross of Jesus is a dramatic symbol of God's Self-revelation. God did not throw us terrible sinners to our knees with a display of judgmental power. Rather, he opened to us his bleeding heart and lovingly invited us to listen, respond, and choose freely to turn from our sin and be made wonderfully new. Rather than the threat of hell came a gentle invitation to holiness. Our freedom to choose was not violated, our dignity as persons not overrun. For the sake of our salvation, love takes the costly risk of being rejected.

The twelve disciples of Jesus sometimes came to him to settle arguments among themselves. He demonstrated for them the holy way to work through debates and differences. Rarely did he give anyone a straightforward answer that made one person right and another wrong. Instead, he asked responding questions that required discernment and spiritual growth. He was a specialist in exercising holy conversation. Holy living is not only about *what* we do, but *how*, and *why*, and *with whom* we do it.

John Wesley considered this sort of holy conversation a potential "means of grace" because conferring with each other—openly, honestly, with mutual respect and concern—opens all involved to more of God's truth and grace, to more of God's people, to more of God's future. Reading the Bible should include inviting to our reading sides that great "cloud of witnesses" (Heb. 12:1) whose lives and legacies of faith and study reverberate across time, geography, and cultures. To read *in community* is a learning discipline, a holy exercise, an enriched conversation. It is one in which the Holy Spirit guides us into truth and calls for internal adjustment as together we seek more understanding and encouragement. Wesley advised new believers to confer with mature believers, sometimes in groups, even listening to opponents and critics.[86] Exercise well by backing away from being arrogant, defensive, and isolated. Become determined to call more real "meetings."

The writer to the Hebrews tells us to "encourage one another daily...so that none of you may be hardened by sin's deceitfulness" (3:13). Accordingly, the Wesley brothers organized a "holy club" for such encouragement, and later started "class meetings" for similar purposes. The church regularly develops small groups of various kinds as more intimate settings for serious conversation on spiritual matters. Such places are where all participants are to be accepted as real persons of worth, even when opinions differ and maturity levels vary. To share openly and listen intently is a valuable holy exercise.

3. **Join the Choir.** As you exercise the discipline of fasting and relate constructively in real conversations, do not forget to sing. The question is not whether you happen to have a good singing voice or a well-developed skill in reading music. If your heart hopes to beat with the spiritual richness of the Hebrew heritage, you need to accept the open invitation to join the Psalmist's choir.

The Book of Psalms is a rich spiritual treasure waiting to be explored, prayed and sung. Rehearsals of this choir are always scheduled when you are taking a serious time out (fasting) or engaged in a serious conference with others on the spiritual journey (or engaging in another of the "means of grace"). Whatever the need or spiritual frontier, there are psalms that word it well.

As you sing, remember that you are in a choir, a member of God's struggling and rejoicing people. Unfortunately, the modern world has moved God off to the side, elevating individuality as the ultimate value—me, my rights, my integrity and fulfillment. The goal, even sometimes in the church, is no longer *shalom*, the grand Hebrew concept of wholeness and well being within the faith community; the goal now is tolerance—we must all be given our space and learn to put up with each other while our personal needs are being met. Otherwise, the threat is that I will leave and go to a better place. Speaking musically, the conductor has been removed from the podium and all members of the choir are acting like soloists. What results can hardly be called music.

One prominent biblical scholar has shown how a believer's spiritual journey goes through three stages, and how the three clusters of the 150 biblical psalms reflect in their distinctive ways the feelings, perceptions, agonies, and joys that characterize all aspects of the journey of faith. Wherever a believer is on the journey and whatever is being faced, there are psalms that understand, put into words, and show the way through. They pray our deepest longings, vent our strongest feelings, and sometimes shout our highest praises. I have charted my own experiences with these stages in Appendix G of my autobiography, calling it "The Christian's Journey to Joy."[87]

The body of Isaac Watts (d.1748) lies in the old cemetery opposite John Wesley's City Road Church in London, England. In 1719 Watts published his book titled *Psalms of David Imitated in the Language of the New Testament*. It includes his hymn "From All that Dwells Below the Skies" (a paraphrase of Psalm 117). He also adapted Psalm 98 to compose the beloved song "Joy to the World!" Following his lead, most modern hymnals include two or three dozen hymns based on the Psalms. This is a great spiritual resource not to be neglected in private or public worship. If you cannot sing them, then think them, hum them, pray them, somehow live with and learn from them. It is great spiritual exercise.

One contemporary body of Christians, the Reformed Presbyterian Church of North America, directs its members to sing only from a psalter in worship services.[88] The members—reflecting their Scottish heritage—judge that this helps to guarantee the biblical authenticity of worship. I recall with gratitude many formal occasions during my years at Geneva College (the fine "RP" school) when we began by singing this from Psalm 100: "All people that on earth do dwell, Sing to the Lord with cheerful voice; Him serve with fear; His praise forth tell; Come ye before Him and rejoice!" It was spiritually rich. I call you to such song. Whether or not you use musical instruments, be sure that your heart is in the singing.

CHAPTER 11

ESPECIALLY WHEN IT HURTS

The grass withers, the flower fades, when the breath of the Lord blows upon it; surely the people are grass. The grass withers, the flower fades; but the word of our God will stand forever (Isaiah 40:7-8).

Then Jesus told his disciples, "If any want to become my followers, let them deny themselves and take up their cross and follow me" (Matt. 16:24).

The combination of "rejoice" and "suffered" in Colossians 1:24 is a strange one, but these are the twin realities to which Paul testifies.... Whenever one serves the church boldly by trying to establish its faith, save it from errors, and widen its borders, at least there will be friction and usually some sacrifice that will involve suffering of one kind or another.... Even so, to suffer in the service of Christ should be seen as a personal privilege.... This cross-life is to become a cross-shaped people in today's secular world.[89]

Karl Marx was just wrong. Christianity, at least when lived as it should be, is not a mere opiate that helps people run away from the real world. When Jesus was breathing his last, he was speaking words of forgiveness. When heading toward the cross, he did anything but run away from trouble. Suffering had to be faced and a world redeemed. His disciples would have to learn that true faith shines forth especially when it hurts.

I have never been much of a jogger, and my interest in doing such running lessens even more each time one of them struggles past me. While I am gently walking along, I see the tense face and hear the grasping for breath. It seems like self-torture being endured for a supposedly good cause. Does medicine have to taste bad, and does exercise have to hurt? Word on the street is this—when it begins to hurt, it is beginning to help. Maybe joggers are smarter than I am. I hope not. I've already caught my breath and I don't want to lose it again.

"No pain, no gain" is hardly a comfortable way to go—and who does not like comfort? But maybe a little suffering is inevitable. Maybe along the spiritual journey suffering is to be expected, and can even be a sign of progress. Maybe. What Jesus says about having to take up a cross is not encouraging.

A Dreamer's Death?

Big changes can happen in life, and they must along the spiritual journey. There is one essential movement of change that surely is more difficult than other forms of strenuous spiritual exercising. It is the struggle to move from sorrow to joy, from experienced loss to anticipated gain, from denial of the difficult to its acceptance by faith. In 1973 James Macholtz, a faculty colleague of mine, wrote a book titled *How to Be a Winning Loser*. Long ago, the psalmist offered a similar promise, the possibility of this progress: "Weeping may stay for the night, but rejoicing comes in the morning"

(Psalm 30:5). We dream of that morning when in the midst of pain—and we try to keep our faith strong in the process.

I was born near Pittsburgh, Pennsylvania, an historic giant of the coal and steel industries. Vast seas of bituminous coal in the area were transformed into mountains of coke, and steel was produced to manufacture the household machines, cars, bridges, and buildings of our recent times. Here is one steelworker's point of view: "It takes uncommon talent, a strong body, and a mind that knows no fear to be able to transform piles of red dirt and scrap into the molten metal that is poured, rolled, and pounded into the various shapes that support the mainframes of civilization."[90] To be a real Christian requires many of the same qualities.

The Pittsburgh that my father's generation knew so well from the 1930s into the 1970s was an industrial giant, but also a smoky, grimy city some called "Hell with the lid off." Then came the big change. In the 1980s forty major industrial plants closed, there were massive redevelopment efforts, and then in 1985 Rand McNally called Pittsburgh "the most livable city in the United States." What a change! It was the fresh morning of a very new day for the city.

One particular Sunday morning was certainly crucial for the very existence of the Christian faith. It was such a dramatic change. The confused and disillusioned disciples of Jesus at first thought of his cross experience as a tragic end to what had been a great prophet's life. Shortly, however, came the resurrection morning and everything suddenly had to be rethought in its bright light. If Hell had its lid off at the cross, Heaven had been unleashed in the garden where the tomb was now empty. What had been "the wooden instrument of a dreamer's death" had become "the supreme altar of the Christian faith."[91] The disciples slowly came to understand the hard but holiest of truths. The cross actually had been the dramatic act of God's Self-revelation and redeeming love. It had to be because of who God is.

In those last days of his life, Jesus had exercised patience and self-control, foregoing the help of heaven to avoid the awful suffering (Matt. 26:53). It could not be avoided or his mission would have failed. Only through Self-giving could the heart of God be revealed as it truly is. It took great hurt to bring us great help. The Father God had exposed on that cross his gracious heart. It bled, withstood undeserved suffering, and reached lovingly and savingly toward all fallen humans, even the ones who were sure that they had ended the life of his Son. For Christians, ultimate Reality had been laid bare on that cross. God is the One who was bending down in suffering and pouring out his heart of love.

To be Christian is to know this helping through hurting. It is to yield gratefully to this amazing insight and come to live in a like manner. To be cross people ourselves and to be so intentionally is surely what it means to be holy as God is holy. To be the church is to be people of the Spirit of the Self-giving Christ, a "community whose presence depends entirely on the presence and power of the Holy Spirit who. . .enables the church effectively to bear witness to Jesus Christ and to be incorporated into his body in every aspect of her life."[92]

Knowing that the cross of Jesus is God's heart unveiled is incredible good news for all who are lost, suffering, guilty, and love-starved. And here is even more good news: Whatever life brings us, if we are faithful to the presence and power of the Holy Spirit, pain can and will move to praise, loss to laughter, salty tears to streams of ever-flowing and living water. On one Friday, the

> *One Sunday morning was certainly crucial for the very existence of the Christian faith. The confused and disillusioned disciples of Jesus at first thought of his cross experience as a tragic end to what had been a great prophet's life. Shortly, however, came the resurrection morning and everything suddenly had to be rethought in its bright light. If Hell had its lid off at the cross, Heaven had been unleashed in the garden where the tomb was now empty.*

sky blackened and Jesus died. On the following Sunday morning, light dawned and word of the resurrection arrived. Love was victorious. Pain was and is not permanent. God is the Suffering Servant—and also the King of kings and Lord of lords!

Holiness is love reigning in the heart, a love that neither denies suffering nor is overcome by it. Holiness has a way of stabilizing life even when it appears out of control. But whatever the gained stability, the holy life is also and always a way of suffering. This must be faced. Those perfected in love hardly seek pain or volunteer for martyrdom, but neither do they flee in fear when such things come. Love has its real risks, and it also has the risen Lord Jesus and the Comforter who promises never to leave us unguided or unprotected or uncomforted (Matt. 28:20).

The death of Jesus was not the disillusioning end of a famous but only fanciful dreamer. It actually was the beginning of the arrival of the kingdom of God, the age yet to come it its glorious fullness. What will be later on can now be realized in significant part through God's love coming to reign in our hearts. Such present realization is what we call holiness.

Look Out!

I had an Old Testament professor in college who made us memorize Isaiah 53 and write this biblical chapter in full from memory on the final exam. He judged it the most important chapter in the Jewish scriptures because it envisions both the sure coming and the surprising nature of the Messiah. And what is the nature of this coming One? It is not pretty. "He was despised and rejected by others; a man of suffering and acquainted with infirmity; and, as one from whom others hide their faces, he was despised and we held him of no account" (53:3).

Is that a conquering, redeeming Messiah? Is the needed power to be seen in humility and suffering? Yes, the Lord of lords and King of kings would mount a hill holding a horrible cross and then be the One who would ask his disciples to follow him on a similar journey of self-sacrifice. Do you want to be holy in the Jesus-way? Popularity, safety, and prosperity will have to be sacrificed.

To follow Jesus requires becoming like Jesus in his humility, self-giving, and pain. Jesus will not tell you to stretch out on a soft bed and nap your way through life on your way to Heaven. He will ask you to engage in difficult exercise, to do nothing less than strain your muscles by taking up your own cross (Matt. 16:24-25). We should not be put off by the irony of it all. Winning in life is found along the painful path of vulnerable loving. In exercise terms, use it or lose it! Activate your call to selfless service or wither away. To be holy is to be open to hurt—and in the process to become aware of joy unspeakable.

The president of the seminary from which I was about to graduate addressed my class and said something that caught our attention big-time (exactly his intent). He said, "I hope that, ten years into your ministries, each of you will be able to report several ministry failures! If you can do that, I will know that you have been on the front lines with God, risking, experimenting, willing to lose in order to occasionally make great strides ahead." That was hardly a welcome prospect, but it was full of holy wisdom.

The year 2012 ended on difficult notes. The United States was said to be going over a "fiscal cliff," super-storm Sandy had just done billions of dollars of damage to the New York City area, and a gunman had bolted into an elementary school in Connecticut and shot to death twenty first-graders and several adult employees, creating shock and outrage across the nation. At the same time, I had just survived a bout with cancer, had taken a good friend to a cancer center for yet another of his painful treatments, and had another good friend whose son was battling with his own life-threatening disease while his daughter was going through an ugly divorce.

There was even more loss than that. Word was out that an ancient Mayan calendar had projected the end of the world before 2013 arrived.

Given the publication date of this book, either that calendar was wrong or we were misreading it. The world of 2012 was witnessing millions of America's young trying to enter a volatile employment world while more millions of the older generations were mourning the loss of earlier dreams, relationships, and careers. Health and vocation get compromised, and sometimes even faith falters in the trauma of it all.

Loss! Look out for it. We all see it come in one form or another, sooner or later. It begins when we are pushed out of the safety of the womb and then it never seems to end—until we finally quit the rhythm of breathing altogether. Loss brings grief, fear, and—if we allow it—resignation, anger, and isolation. The biblical word is that holiness does not protect us from all of this; instead it gives strength, comfort, and vision adequate to see us through. Even so, many of us, rather than accepting holiness as the only real answer, develop selfish defense mechanisms in order to cope. We hide, become unreal and even hypocritical. When we do this, Karl Marx is right—our faith functions as an opiate to keep us asleep and useless and to create illusory fantasies for the poor.

One common fear of such hiding, so unlike Jesus, is that we will be exposed, that people will learn who we really are under the masks we wear for self-protection. Such exposure would bring the pain of public shame that many people do not think they could survive. Any counselor, however,

> *Knowing that the cross of Jesus is God's heart unveiled is incredible good news for all who are lost, suffering, guilty, and love-starved. And here is even more good news. Whatever life brings us, if we are faithful to the presence and power of the Holy Spirit, pain can and will move to praise, loss to laughter, salty tears to streams of ever-flowing and living water.*

knows well that a fear must be faced and recognized for what it is. Once you have honestly faced your hidden or denied self, there will be no more fear of exposure. You will become free to admit and even rejoice in who you really are. When this happens you are now ready to withstand whatever pain is necessary and pay whatever social price is required on the road to honesty and freedom—and holiness.

Paul seems to say that this freedom road is an advanced stage of spiritual growth: "If I must boast, I will boast of the things that show my weakness" (2 Cor. 11:30). Proud of pain? Paul's intent is not really to encourage boasting or being prideful but gaining a sense of freedom that allows us to be who we really are in Christ, weak and yet so strong, confident whether we are understood and appreciated by others or not. Pain and loss come, but, once really in Christ, they can only inflict a soon-passing hurt.

Jesus pointed to the necessity of his followers choosing—yes, choosing—a difficult way that risks misunderstanding and persecution and even a cross. He told his disciples to deny themselves and take up a cross. Where is the gain in this dramatic kind of loss? The Master added: "For those who want to save their life will lose it, and those who lose their life for my sake *will find it*" (Matt 16:25). How ironic—power is made perfect in weakness. Testifies Paul, "For when I am weak, then I am strong" (2 Cor. 12:9-10).

Here is the way of holy breathing, the Jesus-way of finding and fulfilling true life: It involves exhaling our pride and safety mechanisms and inhaling a new self that is formed in the image of Christ. Jesus died, and yet he soon caught the new breath of God's Spirit—resurrection. We are to be his and walk down this same path, catching our breath again by taking in God's ever-living Spirit.

Look out! Loss will come. But if you choose the selfless and voluntary loss suggested by Jesus, life will also come. When it does, it will be a life that can face pain and learn not to cause pain for others. A great example of this special life was featured in a little book that sold millions of copies and caused plenty of controversy.[93] A minor biblical character at best, it is reported that Jabez was born in pain—and his mother gave him a name meaning "pain" (1 Chron. 4:7-10). Can you imagine a mother today naming a child "Nausea" because she was sick during the pregnancy? The Hebrews commonly named children in relation to relevant characteristics or events related to their beginnings.

Jabez, once grown, calls on the God of Israel to bless him and enlarge his territory, to get him beyond the curse of his unfortunate name, to stop the cycle of pain by allowing him to live life to the full, a life that does not cause pain for others. He did not want to pass on the pain as victims of abuse often do by victimizing others. Pain not processed is pain likely passed on. It either is transformed or transmitted. The prayer of Jabez was for a divine blessing that would allow this poor man to become a source of great blessing for others.

This prayer of Jabez was a holiness prayer, the exercise of stretching beyond the pain to the possibility. "Dear God, release me from selfishness to a larger territory where I have room to love others. Bless me so that I can become a blessing to others. Rather than a conveyor of pain, let me be a source of joy!" Praying like this is a spiritual exercise recommended for all believers.

> *Loss! Look out for it. We all see it come in one form or another, sooner or later. It begins when we are pushed out of the safety of the womb and then it never seems to end–until we finally quit the rhythm of breathing altogether. Loss brings grief, fear, and–if we allow it–resignation, anger, and isolation. The biblical word is that holiness does not protect us from all of this; instead it gives strength, comfort, and vision adequate to see us through.*

When we wounded humans dare to exercise like Jabez, stretching for the better and catching the bigger breath of God, seeking more territory to be blessed by God through us, something precious and life-transforming appears. We discover that "the sacred connection can grow stronger *through*, not in spite of, our anxieties, wounds, disappointments, struggles, and needs. The Compassionate One is our gracious friend, and we don't have to earn anything, deserve anything, achieve anything, or merit anything to bring our needs to God. We can come just as we are."[94] Where pain abounds, grace can much more abound!

Mourning and Planting

Our biggest life issue is not the experience of loss. We all will face that. The really big issue is how loss is handled. Some handle difficult things much better than others. Denial or anger may be common and understandable in the face of loss, but both are destructive. What needs to be exercised is the pain of deep mourning and, coming with it, the courage to risk, stretch, and do new planting. Jesus explained to his disciples that a seed is of no value for the future unless it is put in a "death" position (John 12:24). Only then can it manage an amazing rebirth.

Paul offered this instruction to the church at Philippi. Having the same attitude as did Jesus, we should make of ourselves "nothing," taking "the very nature of a servant," being obedient to "even death on a cross." Why? In order that we might come to know something of being "exalted to the highest place," as was Jesus. My old professor was right. Isaiah 53 is worth memorization—and imitation.

The painful path to the holy life has been described well by Henri Nouwen. He says that "mourning and dancing are part of the same movement of grace."[95] We must face painful loss head-on and deliberately connect our suffering with that of the world around us. The holy life is the choice to exercise "compassion," an active entering into the larger community of suffering. We must allow others to help carry our pain, and then we must reach out to carry the pain of others.

ESPECIALLY WHEN IT HURTS

The experience of holiness involves a breathing out and in, first out by releasing the death grip of pain and then in with expressions of love for others in pain. This is truly holy exercise. In this spiritual breathing process there comes a receiving and then a sharing of hope for a new tomorrow. The hope is rooted in a choice to join God in the great work of redemption. The big biblical story, after all, is mostly about God breathing out and then in, accepting the pain of our sin, hanging it on a cross for all to see, and then drawing us in toward himself with the fresh oxygen of new Spirit-life.

The New Testament makes clear that the holy lives of Jesus' followers will be wonder-full, even if not pain-free. Christians will suffer in this world, but the suffering will be a sharing in the sufferings of Jesus—maybe even an experiencing of the baptism of blood that will usher persecuted believers into the heavenly feast of the coming better world (1 Peter 4:12-5:11). No matter. It is a participation in God's life and work and future.

When we engage in the necessary movement that takes us beyond mere "religion" to a vital Christian spirituality, to a deeper and more mature life in God that is the sacred arena of the holy, there will come a wonderful liberation. It is the freedom to focus on *being*, not merely the drive to gain status in God's eyes by *doing*. It is a release from the religious pressure to achieve. We become more aware of the reality of the by-grace journey and the freedom it floods into us. Note this wise testimony of a dear friend of mine:

> For me, it was a delightful awakening when I slowly became aware that my walk with the Lord need not be an uptight, screwed down, perfectionistic, human effort to *do right*. Thankfully, I learned about grace! Really, I think I'm a better person now, a healthier, more effective minister, and I enjoy life more. I am learning to accept the process. I am learning to accept myself as human and fallible. I daily rely on grace, and I

deeply believe God loves me "just as I am." In fact, I may not be as "religious" as I once was, but I believe I'm more spiritual.[96]

The "more spiritual" of this kind is holiness. Exhale the drive to be good enough—you never will be; inhale the grace that receives you in love just as you are, fills your heart with love, and launches you into a life of loving.

Holiness is hardly becoming super-religious. As my friend learned, being more "spiritual" may mean being less "religious." The freedom of holiness is more than release from the need to achieve. It also is stopping the drive of needing to succeed and control. I found it most liberating when I first realized that my Christian calling does *not* include my being responsible for the success of all my efforts for God. I am called to be faithful, regardless of the maze of conflicting and obstructing circumstances. But, in the long run, success is *God's business*. Following our exercise of faithfulness should come a sweet rest in God's faithfulness.

These words of New Testament instruction must be taken in context or they will be tragically misleading. God has given us "a spirit of power and of love and of self-discipline" (2 Tim. 1:7). Love and self-discipline, yes, but power? Are we to wield control and conquer with special divine weapons? Yes, we are, but only with weapons of love, and only as humble servants of the man who chose the cross rather than grasping the temptations of the evil one in the desert. The gifts given by the Spirit are to be used only to heal and build (1 Cor. 12:7). As you mourn, plant. As you receive, give. In your pain, know that new health already is being born. When you are losing your breath, know that soon you will catch it again!

Winning When Losing

What is the holy way of being a real Christian?[97] It is being part of the upside-down kingdom of God, the kingdom of unusual directions and surprising exercises. We win by losing; we stand tall by kneeling down;

we exhale knowing that God will help us catch our breath again. The Christian way is *not* upward mobility, the glitter of success in which our world is so invested. Rather, it is the very opposite, the path of pain, the choice of downward mobility. It is the way that ends on a cross—which, ironically, is the door to resurrection and eternal life. What is Christian leadership? It is not the business of power and control in the usual worldly senses, "but a leadership of powerlessness and humility in which the suffering servant of God, Jesus Christ, is made manifest."[98]

Why did many of the first-century Jews reject Jesus as their Messiah? In large part, it was because they could not accept the strange idea that their "Savior" had been hanged in humiliation by the hated Romans. Are pain and death not signs of sickness and failure? Paul announced a hard truth to the Philippian church. God "has graciously granted you the privilege not only of believing in Christ but of suffering for him as well" (Phil. 1:29).

Suffering—a privilege? Exactly. Reports Peter, "If you endure when you are beaten for doing wrong, what credit is that? But if you endure when you do right and suffer for it, you have God's approval. For to this you have been called because Christ also suffered for you, leaving you an example, so that you should follow in his steps" (1 Peter 2:20-21).

> *What is the holy way of being a real Christian? It is being part of the upside-down kingdom of God. We win by losing; we stand tall by kneeling down; we exhale knowing that God will help us catch our breath again. The Christian way is not upward mobility, the glitter of success in which our world is so invested, but the path of pain, the choice of downward mobility. It is the way that ends on a cross—which, ironically, is the door to resurrection and eternal life.*

Experiencing the joy of faith in Jesus Christ involves a special responsibility and a deep assurance. Jesus tells his disciples essentially this: "Your mission, should you choose to accept it, is to be the salt of the earth" (Matt. 5:13-26). Salt is an active force that adds zest to the world. It brings a needed excitement and hope and endurance that allow real joy to be seen in action. It enhances and preserves life even in tragic circumstances.

In the England known by John Wesley, and very much in our own time and places, a sordid circumstance is that so many people are living in poverty and prisons. Wesley became known as a theologian *of experience*. This does not mean that he was encouraging believers to go from one emotional high to another despite the cautions of reason and the pressing needs of the fallen world around them. What he did mean was that believers are to be immersed in the actual living out of their faith by experiencing God's grace, realizing that it is intended for all, and ministering as healers in the streets, alleys, prisons, and sick-rooms of this world. True holiness is "social" holiness.

To understand poverty requires spending time with the poor, actually feeling and identifying with the pain and doing something about it![99] Ministry for Jesus takes experience and demands exercise. Without the practice of visitation, the nerve of compassion is cut. In his sermon "On Zeal," Wesley went so far as to say that visiting the sick and imprisoned is a *means of grace*—that is, loving service to the sick and impoverished becomes a path of growth and joy for the server as well as the served.

Holiness is not avoiding or denying or being delivered from all of life's pain. The presence of the Lord in our lives actually sends us into the pain as carriers of healing and hope. Such involvement, especially with the poor and desperate, brings a vision and power that rise above circumstances. It brings an assurance and relaxation not of this world. It is a spiritual stretching followed by a contented resting, an exhaling of selfish indulgence and then an inhaling of the fresh air of giving oneself away—a loss that brings the special joy of great spiritual gain.

ESPECIALLY WHEN IT HURTS

The years 1828 to 1910 saw one Russian man create a spiritual tradition that would have a profound effect on Alexander Solzhenitsyn in Russia, and also on men with last names like Gandhi in India and King in the United States. The famous Russian was Leo Tolstoy and his famous writings include *War and Peace*, *Anna Karenina*, and *The Kingdom of God Is Within You*. When communism sought to stamp out Christianity in the decades after Tolstoy's death, the memory of his life and writings helped keep the faith alive.

Tolstoy had a mixed relationship with the Christianity he knew. He found organized religion hollow because of its superstitions and collaborations with oppressive secular power. He resisted false gods inside and outside the church, something that brought him into conflict with both. He became a "radical" follower of Jesus who was the master radical insisting that real life is *in the Spirit*, not in affluence, power, the egotistical search for happiness, or even organized religion. The answer to life's biggest questions is universal love as seen in the Sermon on the Mount, making true Christianity more than a religion, but a sacrificial way of life.

Born to privilege, Tolstoy struggled to free himself from the urges of the flesh and the "natural" desire to enjoy his social advantages that easily thrive at the expense of others. For him, the spiritual perfection—holiness—envisioned in the Gospels of the New Testament cannot come through good works or revolutionary changes in corrupt societies. What then is appropriate and possible in this life? It is "aspiring after this perfection, as individual pilgrims passing through this world, that our intrinsically imperfect natures can be redeemed...and the world be made a happier, more just and more brotherly place to live."[100]

What lies at the heart of true Christian faith? The heart is in the struggle, pain, and sometimes conflict with civil and even religious authorities. It is in the determination to live by faith and not just theorize about it behind sacred walls. It is in the willingness to sacrifice privilege and be out of step with the world. Winning involves losing. Holiness is an exercise in receiving and then sharing hope—hope available in all circumstances and to be shared with those living in the worst of circumstances. It is winning in the midst of losing.

Compassion expands the soul, drives one into the world, and also faces its limits. Holiness is hope that stretches beyond what any of us is able to fully understand or get done on our own. Pope John XXIII is said to have prayed this when retiring at night in the Vatican: "Well, Lord, it's your Church. You take care of it. I'm going to bed." That was not irresponsibility. It was the breathing in of God's amazing and reassuring grace! It was a holiness marked by restfulness, a "holy hush" that only the faithful ever come to know. It outlasts present pain and reaches to the future that only God can provide.

The only real answer to suffering is to look beyond the present pain and clutter of life and get things in a much larger frame. We must learn to hold still, look farther, breathe deeper, and experience the holy hush. One young man managed this when he was on a youth outing with church friends. At one point he got a little separation from the group and stretched out on the ground, couched his head in his hands, and looked up quietly into the immense night sky. The ground was hard and there were persistent and annoying mosquitoes, but something else began to happen. He began to feel like the Creator of everything was looking back from that black eternity and actually noticing tiny little him. His later testimony is truly moving.

"I had this feeling of being seen. Known. Named. Loved. By a Someone bigger than the sky that expanded above me.... It was as if the whole sky were an eye, and all space were a heart, and I was being targeted as a focal point for attention and love." He observes that in the eye of a storm there is the quiet, slow-motion place that can only be described as holy. It is where there is peace that goes beyond understanding. It is the moment of quietness in a world of turmoil, and "in that suspended moment we breathe in *wonder*, and we breathe out *behold*." We still may not be able to explain, but we more deeply understand without having explanations. The pain seems to ease as we breathe in the wonder of God and exhale pure praise.

On another occasion this same man again found himself lost in holy meditation, later reporting: "My thoughts were like a flock of birds flying overhead. They floated by, floated by, and then they were gone. All I could feel was a joyful stillness surrounding me, a clarity cooling me, a peace breathing into me."[101] There it is, bigger than life and basic to life. Especially when we hurt, we must find the eye of the storm, the holy center place, the quiet slow-motion place, the place where we get lost in wonder, where we breathe in the gentle wind of the Spirit and then breathe out our testimony—"behold, my God!"

CHAPTER 12

EMBRACING THE BEYOND

> The power of the age to come was being poured out upon the church for the accomplishment of a universal proclamation...in word and power and demonstration of the Spirit.... The vivid presence of the Spirit heightened expectation, propelled into mission, enlivened worship, and increased consecration in preparation for the appearance of the Lord of the harvest.[102]

> No, it cannot be; none shall live *with* God but he that now lives *to* God; none shall enjoy the glory of God in heaven but he that bears the image of God on earth; none that is not saved from sin here can be saved from Hell hereafter; none can see the kingdom of God *above* unless the kingdom of God be in him *below*.[103] Catch your breath now so that you can breathe forever!

Much is said in the two classic quotations above. What someday will be because of God's good grace has already come—at least in part. The Spirit of God is breathing now on the faithful, who must catch this breath and begin preparing for the final appearance of the Lord of the harvest. If we expect eternal life *then*, we must receive and begin living it *now*.

Circumstance and Vision

It was an especially moving scene, more dramatic than the usual pep talk in the dressing room of a victorious professional football team fresh off the field of conquest. It was not that the young Indianapolis Colts had just won their fifth game in eight tries, and with their hall-of-fame quarterback, Peyton Manning, now gone to another team. The drama was from the victories and much more. It also was that the team's seriously ill new head coach, Chuck Pagano, was standing in their midst pouring out his grateful heart.

When this 2012 season had barely started, Pagano had been stricken with leukemia and already had lost weight and most of his hair from the harsh treatments. But today he had been able to watch the game in person and now was greeting the team behind closed doors. He could not coach, at least not yet, but he could be there on this day, surrounded by his still-sweating team. He was saying to them with a rare passion that he now was living a *vision* rather than being trapped in a *circumstance*.

The cameras were rolling and Pagano's words would be heard again and again on national television in coming days. He was saying with tears in front of strong and transfixed men that he was determined to live on, to dance one day at the weddings of his daughters, and hold high the championship trophy when his team fulfilled its Super Bowl vision. The men stood around him in silence like a crowd of wide-eyed children and then, when he finished, yelled approval and applauded with a fired determination of their own that brought tears everywhere. The coach would win in life—and so would they in their sport. It was in their hearts and one day it would be true on a field of victory.

This electric scene echoes the theological attitude of John Wesley—often called an "optimism of grace." The sinful and death-full *circumstance* of this world appears stacked high against the victory of goodness, justice, and even life itself. The *vision*, however, shines a bright light and braces for the brighter day now expected by true believers. The vision is of God's will, power, grace, and assumed future victory. Suffocation is everywhere these days. However, we are being given the opportunity to catch our breath! It can be in the end as it was in the beginning: "Then the Lord God formed man from the dust of the ground, and breathed into his nostrils the breath of life" (Gen. 2:7).

The promised dance of joy must exist right now if it ever will become reality then. Seeing God's kingdom above requires first committing to the kingdom below. And it can break out now because of belief in the total success of good and right that surely will come one day. Christians who are truly alive, who have caught the eternal breath of the Spirit, are enabled to abide, endure, and hope *now*—regardless of circumstance. To be holy is to exercise hope—no matter what. It is to embrace the beyond and then exhibit its first-fruits right where we are.

> *A holy believer is one who is Spirit-full and faithful in the meantime. Put another way, life is breathing, God's Spirit is blowing, and God's grace is making possible the catching of our eternal-life breath. To breathe in God's Spirit is necessarily to live out God's life.*

Faithful in the Meantime

The key question is this: What about the time between now and then? There will be a day when faith will be sight, when all that now is partial will be whole, when all that now is wrong will somehow be righted. But what about until then? We who follow Jesus and live in and by his Spirit are to anticipate by faith that glorious future and we are to taste and bless others with something of that future glory right now. It is God's Spirit who provides a current pledge of what is yet to come (2 Cor. 5:1-5).

As John Wesley warns in the above quote, "None can see the kingdom of God *above* unless the kingdom of God be in him [or her] *below*." Put another way, a holy believer is one who is Spirit-full and *faithful in the meantime*. Put still another way, life is breathing, God's Spirit is blowing, and God's grace is making possible the catching of our eternal-life breath. To breathe in God's Spirit is necessarily to live out God's life.

The pages of the Old Testament rustle with the exciting rumor that the bondage of weary exiles is finally nearing an end. Word was in the wind that return to Jerusalem was not far away. The route home was to be the highway of holiness (Isaiah 40). Similarly, the teaching of Jesus is full of hints that, even if a crucifixion had to be, a shocking resurrection was on the way, eternal life was in the wind, divine possibilities were pulsating regardless of negative circumstances. They were then and they are now.

There is hope, always hope, in the ever-living and ever-lasting God. The Spirit comes to convict of sin and cleanse from all unrighteousness by revealing, forgiving, comforting, and sanctifying (2 Thess. 2:13). The Spirit also awakens, inspires, and fills with "all joy and peace in believing" so that believers might abound in hope (Rom. 15:13)—and hope enables making a real difference in the meantime.

Check carefully God's revealed calendar as presented graphically below. Christmas is basic for the Jesus revelation, but it is not enough on its own. Lent and the crucifixion were essential for our salvation, but not enough on their own. Easter's glorious resurrection is fundamental, but alone it is not enough. Christian faith rests on *five great realities*, first Christmas—Jesus came; and then the Cross—Jesus died; and then Easter—Jesus rose; and finally, and very importantly, Pentecost—Jesus remains with us in the wisdom, power, and present ministry of his Spirit. But that is only four.

There is one more crucial item on the calendar. There also is Advent—the One who has come *is coming again*! To be holy is to see and embrace the whole Christian calendar and live *now* by the enduring hope of *then*. The "now" is the "ordinary time" during which we must grow in grace and serve patiently in hope.

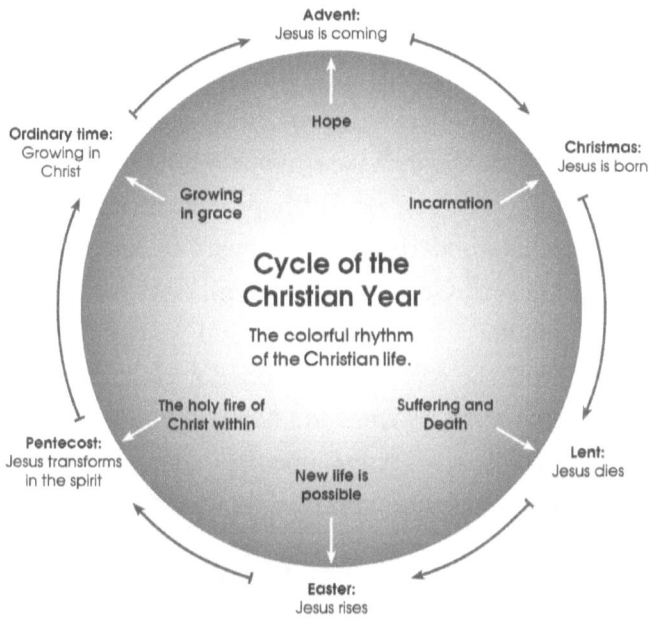

Let me say something that I hope you will quote often. Too many Christians spend their time speculating about when Jesus will come again. They miss something of fundamental importance that enables holy lives in the meantime. At Pentecost, Jesus *already has come again*! The Spirit of the Christ has come *to* us to be *in* us (experienced holiness) in order to move *through* us as ministering love to a broken world (expressed holiness).

To use an exercise image, Christian life is all about *practicing for Heaven*. Heaven is a divine-human union, to be real both now and then. As now, so will it be then. If not now, neither will it be then. Remember the prayer of believers that Jesus taught us? Things should be "on earth as it is in heaven." As now, so then; as here, so there. Holiness delayed is holiness denied. Holiness means finding the joy that comes from living *now* the reality of God's reign in this present age, a reign already come through the ministry of God's Spirit and realized best in the context of today's body of Christ.

When the children of God meet regularly for worship, learning, and service, they naturally form patterns of how they are together. These patterns are sometimes called "liturgy," how the people choose to work together—the "workout" of the people on their way to Christian fullness and faithfulness. They are the holiness exercises that build the group's strength and wisdom and provide the necessary tools for effective church mission.

William Temple (d. 1944), Archbishop of Canterbury, once defined Christian worship this wonderful way: "To worship is to quicken the conscience by the holiness of God, to feed the mind with the truth of God, to purge the imagination by the beauty of God, to open the heart to the love of God, to devote the will to the purpose of God." Here are spiritual practices that have endured all time and cross all borders of church labels and traditions—quicken, feed, purge, open, and devote. They are the very breath of God in action through humble—holy—disciples.

More Than a Future Dream

In 1940 E. Stanley Jones wrote his wonderful little book *Is the Kingdom of God Realism?* His answer to this critical question was a resounding "Yes!" God's reign must be more than the *idealism* of a future dream. It must be translated into the *realism* of current life as God intends and is presently prepared to enable. Communist utopianism was in vogue in 1940; it would not last. By contrast, Christ's vision of the eternal kingdom of God already coming among us was then and is now timely good news. Already well into the twenty-first century, we know that communist utopianism that created a "Cold War" in the 1950s and 1960s is long gone, but Christ's vision of the kingdom of God remains as true as ever.

EMBRACING THE BEYOND

In his book *Falling Upward* Richard Rohr speaks about the matured or holy stage of Christian faith as the second half of life. Darkness remains in various ways, but there has come a changed capacity to hold complex things creatively and with less anxiety. It is what John of the Cross long ago called "luminous darkness." It is the ability to embrace simultaneously both deep suffering and intense joy. In the Wesleyan theological tradition of Christianity, this embracing ability is believed possible because divine grace allows a true loving of God and neighbor.

This optimism of grace ought to energize and make believers anxious to live the Spirit life in every moment—to exhale death in anticipation of one day inhaling that grand moment of Christ's final return. It should bring focus to God's goal, God's intended end for creation. It is nothing less than the transformation of this present age through universal love in preparation for the age yet to come.

However far we have walked down the holiness road, enabled by breathing in God's guiding and transforming Spirit, we humbly know that we are *still in the making*. It is the "sufferings of this present time" (Rom. 8:18-21) that keep us prayerful and Christ-dependent. We are not what we once were, but we are not yet what one day we will be. We long for a final sanctification that will involve a new "body" beyond Paul's ability to describe (1 Cor. 15:35-44). Warmed and fired by this vision and expectation, we press on to the final goal (Phil. 3:10, 12-14).

As we await the fullness and finality of our faith, our waiting has integrity only when it bears good fruit in the meantime. Holiness must be more than a future dream. Effective Christian witness happens best when love and related evidences of the Spirit's present life are very evident in our lives. Announced Dietrich Bonhoeffer, "If you would find *eternity*, give yourself to *time*.... If you desire God, hold fast to the world."[104] He did not mean to be *of* the world, but *for* the world as God's redeeming instruments. To be meaningfully *for* requires getting deeply involved. Holiness is a set-apartness but never a selfish or defensive separateness.

Reggie McNeal is both correct and graphic when he talks about getting involved.[105] Christian people too often reduce the activities of their Christian lives to little more than "the consumption of spiritual goods." They try to be faithful by taking in worship services, giving some money, agreeing to be part of a small study group, etc., mostly all done on church grounds. Consequently, using the imagery of Jesus' parable of the Good Samaritan, they quietly ride right by people in big trouble, hoping not to be late for something or other at the church.

So what does McNeal recommend? Disciples of Jesus, he says, are built for sacrificial service to neighbors, so we must *get off our donkeys* and get into the fray of the world's pain. We are built to serve and must exercise our service muscles or our souls will be severely undernourished and stunted—to say nothing of the injured people lying by the side of the road who hope for some less "religious" person to come along and actually help.

Failing to exercise faith in the marketplaces of this life is to become faith-less, use-less, breath-less. Then will come the divine pronouncement like the one to the church in Laodicea: "I know your works; you are neither cold nor hot. I wish that you were either cold or hot. So, because you are lukewarm, and neither cold nor hot, I am about to spit you out of my mouth" (Rev. 3:15-16). Many Christians are at least lukewarm, saying good things and intending good things—at least someday, like a future dream. Holiness is being touched by the Holy God and then coming alive in loving service—now.

Resurrection is not only a wonderful new aliveness waiting to become reality beyond this world. We can either get stuck in passive resistance to God's mission right here or be revived by passionate engagement in it. Jesus said that "anyone who hears my word and believes him who sent me *has eternal life* [now!], and does not come under judgment, but [already!] has passed from death to life" (John 5:24). The present relevance of this future life with God is crucial.

Three New Testament metaphors point the way, the holy way to be in this world while we are awaiting for the arrival of the next.[106]

1. Commit to the community of faith, the church. God is birthing a people to be a sign of God's work in the world.
2. Church life should be cross-shaped, showing how God chooses to work in this fallen world.
3. Church life is to embody the power of Christ's resurrection, making clear that it is a forerunner of a new creation because the first-fruits of the Spirit are already very evident (Rom. 8:22-23).

When the church is faithful to this holy way, it will be clear to the world that the age to come already has begun to appear. The wind of God that will blow *then* can be felt and breathed in even *now*.

The entire biblical story of God in and for this world focuses in Jesus Christ and reveals a basic truth. It centers in the Spirit of God *carrying forward* that which God has planned from eternity and now has provided in Christ. God wants to save and sanctify a people to be his own holy treasure (1 Peter 2:9). The truth is about a divine community, the church of Jesus. The dramatic pentecostal birth of the church "shifts the scene back and forth from the inner life of personal renewal of individual believers to the church's outer mission of peace, justice, and liberation. The new community of the Spirit, the church, is called to model for the world that which is yet to be."[107]

One with the Whole Church

Christian life, if it is to be an active and relevant and holy life, cannot be an isolated, individualistic affair. We are called into a community of faith that lives by a breath and vision and power not its own. Note this wisdom:

> Clearly scripture presents more than just a set of religious concepts or theological principles. An alternate order of being confronts us. It draws us out of our false self and into a mode of being where our true self is found. The scripture draws us into a community of people across the centuries who have found their true life in this alternate order of being. Through participation in the experience of that community, we come to full understanding of the scripture.[108]

Can and will you take all of this wisdom into your own thinking, believing, breathing, and living? The alternate order of being, eternal life, is the life of God being exercised in the present on the way to the future.

The Bible challenges all believers in Jesus to become part of a divine community (the church) where there is clear evidence of this alternate order of being and where—and only where—we will be able to gain a full understanding of the Bible and the possibilities of a holy existence in a very unholy world.

The second-century manual of church life is commonly known as the *Didache*. It offers this instruction that is as modern as ancient: "Meet together frequently in your search for what is good for your souls." Exercise church! Being will lead to going—mission. Go together, employing the energies of the Spirit. Go to minister in God's name. Such meeting and then going is the truly holy way of being Christian. This way redeems the now on the way to God's future.

From my home church I absorbed the love of good pastoral leadership, an appreciation for nurturing young leaders, and a vision of the church as much more than any flawed human institution of religion. After some years of my own ministry, my spiritual need led me, a committed Protestant, to a Roman Catholic monastery. Beginning in the 1980s I became a periodic Protestant retreatant in a bastion of historic Roman Catholicism. It has been a place that has helped me experience larger dimensions of God's one, holy, catholic church. The vision fostered in my youth has persisted and expanded.

The Abbey of Gethsemani has sat quietly as a spiritual oasis in the hills of rural Kentucky since 1848. It has carried on a ministry of hospitality, providing spiritual retreats characterized by solitude, silence, and Christian reflection. In one way, making this Abbey a spiritual home was quite a turn from my free-church Protestant upbringing (although over the centuries monasteries have been home to numerous Roman "radicals"); in another way, it was part of my growing up into the wider church without denying anything precious from my youth. My home pastor had called for an elimination of denominational walls and a unity of believers based on relationship to Christ. I have been practicing this radical call, following God's sanctifying and unifying Spirit into God's larger body.

> *So much is found when we get lost in God's love. One is wonderfully united in communion with the saints of all time. In a sense, whether or not we die, we are always present to our brothers and sisters. Everyone matters and has influence and is somehow present and not just past. Exercising holiness renders one open, vulnerably open to God and to God's people and creation.*

The monastery environment, contrary to common perception, is not intended to disdain the world—as is made clear in the writings of Thomas Merton (a famous Gethsemani resident). The point of retreat is not to give up, but to prepare to charge into the world. It is an intentional spiritual exercising, a holding still, getting in touch with oneself and God. It is a cherishing of the long tradition of God in the world, actually practicing prayer and God's presence, relishing the sweet sounds of silence, and finally realizing that true value lies first in *being* and only then in *doing*. My book *Authentic*

Spirituality highlights the several historic streams of Christian spirituality, including the contemplative of this monastery. The greatest richness comes in a combination of these streams (see chapter 10), a becoming one with the whole church.

Does my retreating make me a Protestant or a Catholic? Both and neither. I now am a Christian who belongs to the whole church. I protest on occasion and choose to be "catholic" in the broadest sense. I am reaching for the wider stream of Christian riches, benefiting from all and restricted by none. This journey has only begun for me. I am working my way down the highway of holiness. I am a pilgrim still progressing.[109] Nonetheless, at least the corner has been turned and the holy journey is happening. I have my God-issued passport and I am exercising my travel privileges.

In *Falling Upward* Richard Rohr speaks wisely of "deep time," the time when one becomes lost in God's love. In this lostness, so much is found! One is wonderfully united in communion with the saints of all time. Rohr half-teasingly says that this is a good way to think of "reincarnation." In one sense we never die and are always present to our brothers and sisters. In deep time, everyone matters and has influence, and is somehow present and not just past. Exercising holiness renders one open, vulnerably open to God and to God's people and creation. To be truly holy is to be both *open* and *on the way* with all of one's sisters and brothers.

God is touching, calling, forming a people who are distinctive now because they are being enabled to reflect the qualities of the Holy One who has made them a set-apart people and one day will bring them a final wholeness. We can become "holy" only as we participate in God's loving character and become witnesses of the divine will in this world. As Paul puts it, "And all of us, with unveiled faces, seeing the glory of the Lord as though reflected in a mirror, are being transformed into the same image from one degree of glory to another; for this comes from the Lord, the Spirit" (2 Cor. 3:18). Holiness is restoring people to the way they ought to be. Holiness is an invitation to share in the divine character and then participate in the divine mission.

Some have sought to restore holiness to today's churches in a truly biblical way. Note the "Holiness Manifesto" released in 2006 by a cluster of concerned denominational leaders. This well-known statement announces that "there has never been a time in greater need of a compelling articulation of the message of holiness. Pastors and church leaders at every level of the church have come to new heights of frustration in seeking ways to revitalize their congregations and denominations.... Therefore... we set forth for the church's well being a fresh focus on holiness. In our view, this focus is the heart of Scripture concerning Christian existence for all times—and clearly for our time."[110]

The primary intention of God is not merely getting each of us to heaven—no small thing, of course. Rather, it is calling, gathering, centering, and sending a people into the world who will share what it looks like to really live now under the reign of God. The "centering" piece of God's intention is the constant holiness preoccupation of the Bible. We are to be "saved" by Christ's life (Rom. 5:10), saved in the double sense of entering into Christ's eternal kind of life, and not just in some distant heaven but right now in the midst of our broken world.

> *God's coming to us with love and redemption is the Father's "Yes!" in the Son, Jesus Christ. Yes, we are yet loved, never forgotten, recipients of an amazing gift that enables new life and hope that is eternal. Our proper response to such news can only be "Amen!—so be it, yes God, I receive, I breathe in, I cherish, I will be faithful to nurture and employ this gift for the benefit of others."*

The people of the church must become focused on breathing the very breath of God and thus expressing God's present reign. Only then can the church stop being merely a vendor of desired religious goods and services. Instead, it can emerge as a living example of Christ resurrected and the spearhead of God's saving mission—*now*!

Always Say a Holy "YES!"

Many biblical prayers end with flourishes of joy and thanksgiving. There is the dramatic explanation mark of "Amen!" One can sense this ending affirmation in the "Wonderful" or "Yes!" at the end of 2 Timothy 4:18—"The Lord will rescue me from every evil attack and save me for his heavenly kingdom. To him be the glory forever and ever. Amen!"

God's coming to us with love and redemption is the Father's "Yes!" in the Son, Jesus Christ. Yes, we are yet loved, never forgotten, recipients of an amazing gift that enables new life and hope that is eternal. The proper response to such news is to be echoed by our grateful and very affirmative response: "Amen!—so be it, yes God, I receive, I breathe in, I cherish, I will be faithful to nurture and employ this gift for the benefit of others."

When we conclude praying as Jesus said we should (Matt. 6:9-13), we realize that we have laid out before God our very lives. We reach affirmatively to the One who has reached affirmatively to us. Life now becomes committed to hallowing God's name and allowing God's kingdom to come, first in ourselves and always by doing on earth the will of God who is in heaven. We are alive again, holy, set apart, and in our aliveness we will exercise our new privileges and opportunities with joy and thanksgiving.

Things once out of the question now are real opportunities for the championing of the possibilities of God's grace. It is launch time for existence in the Spirit of Christ. It is breathing and exercise time! Praying with Jesus brings us into "God's will and manner of being and living...in the One who sits above time and is in charge of eternity...the One through whom we now live and to whom belongs the glory, for ever and ever. Amen!"[111]

Christian life should be the pursuit of experienced and lived holiness, of the kingdom of God coming in us now. The church should be the gathering of the "saints" for group exercises in joyful thanksgiving to God and grace-enabled growing and serving through the power of God's Spirit. Paul told the Corinthians that "all the promises of God in him [Jesus] are *Yes*, and in Him *Amen*, to the glory of God *through us*" (2 Cor. 1:20).

A woman once said the following about the holiness evangelist E. Stanley Jones: "Apart from the Holy Spirit, Brother Stanley would be a mess." Jones reports this assessment in his autobiography, adding humbly: "But with the Holy Spirit I am not a mess, but a *message*." What a difference![112] Jones was, in fact, a living *Yes* back to the God who had first said *yes* to him.

The great need in the church today is a hearty acceptance of the call for the holiness of God's people. Early lines of Charles Wesley's hymn "Love Divine, All Loves Excelling" express what should be the heart-cry of every earnest believer and congregations:

> Love divine, all loves excelling,
> Joy of heaven to earth come down,
> Fix in us Thy humble dwelling,
> All Thy faithful mercies crown.
> Jesus, Thou art all compassion,
> Pure, unbounded love Thou art,
> Visit us with Thy salvation,
> Enter every trembling heart.

Listen to more words from that 2006 "Holiness Manifesto" written by yours truly and fourteen others representing the Wesleyan Holiness Consortium:

> People in churches are tired of our petty lines of demarcation that artificially create compartments, denominations, and divisions. They are tired of building institutions. They want to

know the unifying power of God that transforms. They want to see the awesomeness of God's holiness that compels us to oneness in which there is a testimony of power. God is holy and calls us to be a holy people.

A key Christian action is saying regularly the right word, the holy word, and living in its affirming wake. Here is one testimony of that word: "So I live in a state of 'Yesness,' Yes to him [the Lord Jesus], primarily and absolutely; Yes to life and its responsibilities; Yes to approaching death; Yes to his everything!"[113]

Are you ready to engage seriously in active holiness exercises, catching the wind of God and actually being God's person in today's world? Hear God's *Yes* that surrounds you and dare to be God's *Yes* to the world. Hearing and daring are essential. They become substantive, they become holy reflections of a holy God only when a series of exercises become your spiritual routine. As my friend Howard Snyder has laid out the five-fold exercise plan:

> Be filled with all the fullness of God in Christ, living holy, devout, pure, healing lives, being Jesus' counter-culture and contrast society in witness to the world;

> Exercise a beautiful and effective array of ministries and callings, according to the diversity of the gifts of the Spirit;

> Be God's kingdom people in the world, living in full allegiance to Jesus and his reign—Spirit-endowed co-workers for the kingdom of God;

> Live as a faithful covenant people, building accountable community, growing up into Jesus Christ, embodying the spirit of God's law in holy love;

> Care for the garden, this good earth, God's gift in trust to us, working in faith, hope and confidence for the healing of all creation, being the leading edge among the nations for the care and feeding and eventual reconciliation of all things... (Eph. 1:10, 22; 3:9; Col. 1:16-20; Heb. 1:2-3).[114]

Here is the essence of Christian holiness—be filled, be co-workers, be faithful, be accountable, be caring, be holy! God's wind is blowing right now. Catch your breath!

ENDNOTES

1. Alain de Botton, *Religion for Atheists: A Non-Believer's Guide to the Uses of Religion* (N.Y.: Vintage Books, 2012), 11-12.

2. Ibid., 12, 145.

3. Don Thorsen, *Calvin vs Wesley: Bringing Belief in Line with Practice* (Abingdon Press, 2013), 56-57.

4. Timothy George, *Theology of the Reformers*, 1988, 224, quoting John Calvin, *Instiutes*, 3.1.1. Emphasis added.

5. John and Charles Wesley, "Groaning for the Spirit of Adoption," *Hymns and Sacred Poems* (1740), st. 1.

6. Barry L. Callen, *Authentic Spirituality* (Emeth Press, 2006), 115-116.

7. William H. Willimon, in Kenneth Collins and John Tyson, eds., *Conversion in the Wesleyan Tradition* (Abingdon Press, 2001), 243.

8. The Shaker community is now a tourist site more than an active religious community.

9. Thomas Merton, *Seeking Paradise: The Spirit of the Shakers* (Orbis Books, 2003), 77.

10. David Elton Trueblood, *While It Is Day* (New York: Harper & Row, 1974), 161-162.

11. Howard A. Snyder, *Yes in Christ* (Clements Publishing, 2011), 100.

12 Verse four of "Spirit Holy, Breathe on Me" by Edwin Hatch and B. B. McKinney.

13 Billy Collins, "Velocity," in *Nine Horses* (Random House, 2002), 11-12.

14 John Westerhoff, *Spiritual Life* (Louisville, KY: Westminster John Knox, 1994), 1.

15 Note the inspired web address of the Wesleyan Holiness Consortium—*HolinessAndUnity.org*.

16 Howard A. Snyder, "Holiness and the Five Calls of God," in Mannoia and Thorsen, eds., *The Holiness Manifesto* (Grand Rapids: Eerdmans Publishing, 2008), 142.

17 See Philip R. Meadows, "'Candidates for Heaven': Wesleyan Resources for a Theology of Religions," in *Wesleyan Theological Journal* (35:1, spring 2000), 99ff.

18 Barry L. Callen, *Beneath the Surface: Reclaiming the Old Testament for Today's Christian* (Emeth Press, 2012), 111.

19 See Thomas Jay Oord and Michael Lodahl, *Relational Holiness* (Kansas City, Beacon Hill Press, 2005).

20 Oord and Lodahl, *Relational Holiness*, 102.

21 Dennis F. Kinlaw, *Prayer: Bearing the World as Jesus Did* (Francis Asbury Press, 2012), 1.

22 Kinlaw, ibid., 7.

23 Billy Collins, "No Time," in *Nine Horses* (Random House, 2002), 101.

24 Carl Jung, *The Structure and Dynamics of the Psyche* (Pantheon Books, 1960).

25 Richard Rohr, *Falling Upward* (Josey-Bass, 2011).

26 Barry L. Callen, *Authentic Spirituality: Moving Beyond Mere Religion* (Baker Books, 2001, Emeth Press, 2006), 136.

27 Richard Rohr, *Falling Upward*.

ENDNOTES

28 William Greathouse, *Love Made Perfect: Foundations for the Holy Life* (Beacon Hill Press of Kansas City, 1997), 8.

29 Charles Wesley, referring to Job 9:20, in *Short Hymns on Select Passages of the Holy Scriptures* (Bristol: Farley, 1762), 1:228.

30 Kevin Mannoia, *Masterful Living: New Vocabulary for the Holy Life* (Aldersgate Press, rev. ed., 2012), 9.

31 Mannoia, *Masterful Living*, 103.

32 John Wesley in &5 of his famous *A Plain Account of Christian Perfection*.

33 Kenneth E. Jones, *Commitment to Holiness* (Anderson, IN: Warner Press, 1985), 167.

34 Oord and Lodahl, *Relational Holiness*, 135.

35 John Wesley, in his "Brief Thoughts on Christian Perfection" (1767).

36 See Barry L. Callen, "Soteriological Synergism and Its Surrounding Seductions," in the *Wesleyan Theological Journal*, 46:2, Fall 2012, 25-40.

37 M. Robert Mulholland, Jr., *Shaped by the Word*, rev. ed. (Upper Room Books, 2000), 75.

38 Michael Lodahl, *The Story of God: A Narrative Theology* (Beacon Hill Press of Kansas City, second edition, 2008), 196.

39 Clark H. Pinnock, *Three Keys to Spiritual Renewal* (Eugene, OR: Wipf & Stock Publishers, 1998), 53.

40 Rueben P. Job, *A Wesleyan Spiritual Reader* (Abingdon Press, 1998), 207.

41 Dietrich Bonhoeffer, *The Cost of Discipleship*, as quoted in Bob and Michael Benson, *Disciplines for the Inner Life* (Word Books, 1985), 157.

42 Cheryl Johnson Barton, *Steady Till Sunset* (Warner Press, 2011).

43 James Earl Massey, *Spiritual Disciplines* (Zondervan, 1985), 46.

44 Alister McGrath, *Beyond the Quiet Time: Practical Evangelical Spirituality* (Grand Raids: Baker, 1995), 11.

45 This feather image is found in the book *Pathway to Our Hearts* by Thomas Collins.

46 Randy L. Maddox, *Responsible Grace: John Wesley's Practical Theology* (Nashville, TN: Kingswood Books, Abingdon Press, 1994), 158.

47 Maddox, *Responsible Grace*, 179.

48 Mannoia, *Masterful Living*, 103-104.

49 Richard Rohr, *Falling Upward*.

50 Barry L. Callen, *Caught Between Truths: The Central Paradoxes of Christian Faith* (Emeth Press, 2007), 107-108, 114.

51 Maddox, *Responsible Grace*, 143.

52 D. Elton Trueblood, *A Place to Stand* (Harper and Row, 1969), chapter one.

53 Mark Buchanan, *Spiritual Rhythm: Being with Jesus Every Season of Your Soul* (Zondervan, 2010), preface, 28.

54 Richard Rohr, *Falling Upward*.

55 A version of this imaginative picture is found in Henri Nouwen, *Our Greatest Gift* (HarperOne, 1994), 19.

56 See Nouwen's *Spiritual Formation: Following the Movements of the Spirit* (HarperCollins e-books, 2010).

57 Henri Nouwen, in *Henri Nouwen: Writings Selected* (Orbis Books, 1998), 6.

58 See John Wesley's sermon titled "Sermon on the Mount: Discourse 2."

59 See William Barclay, *The Mind of St. Paul* (N.Y.: Harper & Row, 1958), chapter ten.

60 John Wesley, in a letter to the Lord Bishop of London, and in his Journal, vol. 1.

61 See the essay "Please Don't Call Me 'Christian'" by Barry L. Callen, found in my autobiography, *A Pilgrim's Progress* (Anderson University Press and Emeth Press, 2008, 2nd ed., 2013), 471-474.

ENDNOTES

62 Clark H. Pinnock, *Flame of Love: A Theology of the Holy Spirit* (InterVarsity Press, 1996), 114.

63 Pinnock, *Flame of Love*, 187.

64 Richard Rohr, *Falling Upward*.

65 Christine D. Pohl, *Making Room: Recovering Hospitality as a Christian Tradition* (Eerdmans Publishing, 1999), 33.

66 Richard Foster, *Streams of Living Water* (HarperSanFrancisco, 1998), 95.

67 John Howard Yoder, "The Hermeneutics of Peoplehood," in *The Priestly Kingdom* (Notre Dame, IN: University of Notre Dame Press, 1984), 24.

68 Brian D. McLaren, *Naked Spirituality* (HarperOne, 2011), 21.

69 James Earl Massey, *Spiritual Disciplines* (Zondervan, 1985), 116.

70 Randy L. Maddox, *Responsible Grace*, 218.

71 See Barry L. Callen, *The Prayer of Holiness-Hungry People: A Disciple's Guide to the Lord's Prayer* (Francis Asbury Press, 2011).

72 See D. Michael Henderson, *John Wesley's Class Meeting: A Model for Making Disciples* (Nappanee, IN: Evangel Publishing House, 1997).

73 See Elaine A. Heath and Scott T. Kisker, *Longing for Spring: A New Vision for Wesleyan Community* (Eugene, Oregon: Cascade Books, 2010).

74 Marvin Wilson, *Our Father Abraham: Jewish Roots of the Christian Faith* (Grand Rapids: Wm. Eerdmans, 1989), 159.

75 Henri Nouwen, *In the Name of Jesus* (N.Y.: Crossroad, 1989), 31-32.

76 George Lyons, in Diane Leclerc and Mark A. Maddix, *Spiritual Formation: A Wesleyan Paradigm* (Beacon Hill Press of Kansas City, 2011).

77 See Clark H. Pinnock and Barry L. Callen, *The Scripture Principle: Reclaiming the Full Authority of the Bible* (3rd ed., Emeth Press, 2009), 189ff.

78 See Barry L. Callen, *Caught Between Truths: The Central Paradoxes of Christian Faith* (Lexington, KY: Emeth Press, 2007).

79   Richard Rohr, *Falling Upward*.

80   David R. Nienhuis, "The Community of Holiness," in Daniel Castelo, ed., *Holiness as a Liberal Art* (Pickwick Publications, 2012), 97, 99.

81   Richard J. Foster, *Streams of Living Water: Celebrating the Great Traditions of Christian Faith* (HarperSanFrancisco, 1998), introduction.

82   James Earl Massey, *Spiritual Disciplines* (Zondervan, 1985), 31.

83   These streams are elaborated in Barry L. Callen, *Authentic Spirituality* (Baker, 2001, Emeth Press, 2006), 71ff, 93ff, 122ff, 147ff, 172ff, and 195ff.

84   See the full Pinnock story in the biography by Barry L. Callen titled *Clark H. Pinnock: Journey Toward Renewal* (Evangel Publishing House, 2000).

85   See Dag Hammarskjöld's 1993 spiritual classic titled *Markings*.

86   Randy L. Maddox, "'Honoring Conference': Wesleyan Reflections on the Dynamics of Theological Reflection," *Methodist Review* 4(2012), 7.

87   Barry L. Callen, *A Pilgrim's Progress: The Autobiography of Barry L. Callen* (Anderson University Press and Emeth Press, 2nd ed. 2013), App. G.

88   See *The Book of Psalms: For Singing* (The Board of Education and Publication, Reformed Presbyterian Church of North America, 1973).

89   Barry L. Callen, in Wilson, Deasley, and Callen, *Galatians, Philippians, Colossians: A Commentary for Bible Students* (Wesleyan Publishing House, 2007), 311-312.

90   Quoted in Laurie Graham, *Singing the City* (University of Pittsburgh, 1998), 65.

91   H. Wheeler Robinson, *The Experience of the Holy Spirit* (N.Y.: Harper and Brothers, 1928), 78.

92   Jason E. Vickers, *Minding the Good Ground: A Theology for Church Renewal* (Baylor University Press, 2011), 36.

93   *The Prayer of Jabez* by Bruce Wilkinson (2000).

94   McLaren, *Naked Spirituality*, 121. Emphasis added.

ENDNOTES

95 Henri Nouwen, *Spiritual Formation*.

96 Dwight L. Grubbs, *Beginnings: Spiritual Formation for Leaders* (Lima, Ohio: Fairway, 1994), 36-37.

97 Note that the biography of John Wesley by Kenneth J. Collins (Abingdon, 1999) is titled *A Real Christian*.

98 Henri Nouwen, *In the Name of Jesus*, 63.

99 Horizon International is a ministry in which I am deeply involved. We serve young African orphaned because by AIDS. Our program features "GO Teams," groups of Americans who go to Africa to see, touch, and help the orphans firsthand. Once people have gone, they usually commit to serious service. See my history of this ministry, *Hope on the Horizon* (2010).

100 Malcolm Muggeridge writing about Tolstoy in *A Third Testament* (Little, Brown and Company, 1976), 171.

101 Brian D. McLaren, *Naked Spirituality* (HarperOne, 2011), 8, 203.

102 Steven J. Land, *Pentecostal Spirituality: A Passion for the Kingdom* (Sheffield, England: Sheffield Academic Press, 1993), 72-73.

103 John Wesley, *Works* (Jackson edition), 10:364, emphasis added.

104 Mary Bosanquet, *The Life and Death of Dietrich Bonhoeffer* (NY: Harper and Row, 1968), 70. Emphasis added.

105 See the book by Reggie McNeal titled *Get Off Your Donkey!* (Baker Books, 2013).

106 These are found in Richard B. Hays, *The Moral Vision of the New Testament* (HarperSanFrancisco, 1996), 193-205.

107 Barry L. Callen, *Faithful in the Meantime: A Biblical View of Final Things and Present Responsibilities* (Nappanee, IN: Evangel, 1997), 264.

108 M. Robert Mulholland, Jr., *Shaped by the Word* (Nashville: Upper Room Books, rev. ed., 2000), 74.

109 See my autobiography titled *A Pilgrim's Progress* (Anderson University and Emeth Presses, 2008, 2013).

110 See the book *The Holiness Manifesto*, eds. Kevin Mannoia and Don Thorsen (Eerdmans Publishing, 2008).

111 See Callen, *The Prayer of Holiness-Hungry People*, 122.

112 See Jones, *Song of Ascents* (Nashville: Abingdon Press, 1968), 26.

113 See Jones, *Song of Ascents*, 316.

114 Howard A. Snyder, "Holiness and the Five Calls of God: Holiness in Postmodernity," in *The Holiness Manifesto*, ed. Kevin Mannoia and Don Thorsen (Grand Rapids: Eerdmans, 2008), 129-151.

www.ingramcontent.com/pod-product-compliance
Lightning Source LLC
Chambersburg PA
CBHW030319080526
44584CB00012B/631